W9-BAF-610

LAUREL
GLEN
San Diego, California

ORCHIDS
a care manual

Brian & Sara Rittershausen

Publishing Director
Alison Goff
Creative Director
Keith Martin
Executive Editor
Julian Brown
Executive Art Editor
Mark Winwood
Design
Rozelle Bentheim
Editor
Karen O'Grady
Production Controller
Sarah Scanlon
Picture Research
Sally Claxton
Photography
Mark Winwood
Illustrations
Martin Jarman

North American Edition
Publisher
Allen Orso
Managing Editor
JoAnn Padgett
Project Editor
Elizabeth McNulty

Laurel Glen Publishing
An imprint of the Advantage Publishers Group
5880 Oberlin Drive, San Diego, CA 92121-4794
www.laurelglenbooks.com

Copyright © 2000 Octopus Publishing Group
Limited

Copyright under International, Pan American, and
Universal copyright. All rights reserved. No part of
this publication may be reproduced, stored in a
retrieval system, or transmitted in any form or by
any means, mechanical, photocopying, recording
or otherwise, without the permission of the
copyright holders.

Library of Congress Cataloging-in-Publication data available on request

ISBN 1-59223-086-5

1 2 3 4 5 07 06 05 04 03
Produced by Toppan
Printed in China

Contents

Introduction

Whether it is an amateur with a few plants on the window sill, the mass production of cut flowers for the florist trade, or the serious hobbyist, the passion for orchids is ever-expanding. All these interests are greatly increasing throughout the world, wherever people like to grow beautiful flowers, and as will be seen on page 12, this interest dates back thousands of years.

Throughout Europe, the earliest apothecaries looked to the plant kingdom for a "cure-all" for the many ailments from which they suffered. They collected the plants of the countryside and described each one in great detail, particularly its medicinal and culinary uses. Among these plants were native, terrestrial orchids, all of which were found to be useful. These early books were often lavishly illustrated with woodcuts and each one painstakingly handwritten; as the scholars were mainly ecclesiastical, the words were always written in Latin.

The written word was gradually superceded by print and so the books became more widely available but only to the chosen few who could read and write. As the literacy of the population improved, so the demand for books increased and when the modern era of orchid growing started, books about orchids became more and more in demand. In Britain, John Bateman published a very large book in 1837 printed on elephant folio, the largest paper manufactured at that time. It illustrated the orchids of Mexico and Guatemala, in life size and splendid color. Such books were produced for limited circulation and today change hands for extremely

large sums of money. Those who are lucky enough to own or just glimpse such a publication will see the colors as bright and true as the day they were printed.

By the end of the nineteenth century there were many orchid books, several encyclopedias, and even a monthly magazine, *The Orchid Review*, first published in 1893 and dedicated entirely to orchids. Today the range of orchid books is enormous; some are definitive publications dealing with one scientific genera while others specialize in the orchids of one particular region or country. The object of this book is to provide a care manual for the amateur or complete beginner who has never grown orchids before and would like more knowledge and help to build their own collection. It is written by a father and daughter whose lifetime of experience is based on serving and supplying orchids to the people for whom this book is intended.

We begin with the natural history of this enormous family of plants, describing their geographical distribution and natural habitats, and also the history of growing these wonderful and diverse plants in cultivation. We then go on to describe in detail how to grow orchids and the conditions under which they will thrive to enable the reader to get the very best results from their

plants. We then discuss the potting of orchids, which composts and pots to use for which plants, and how to go about repotting. Next we describe how to divide a plant and inform the reader about the latest propagation techniques, including seed-sowing, hybridization, and meristem culture. The pests and diseases likely to be encountered along the way are described and illustrated in detail, ending the practical sections of the book.

In the second half, we list and describe the most popular genera of orchids in cultivation today. These are the plants that are most readily available from specialty orchid nurseries, at orchid shows, and some garden centers. With thousands of orchids to choose from, it can be daunting for the beginner to know where to start, the selection that we have listed here is intended to make this task easier. This section is followed by more unusual orchid genera, which are all available and well recommended for the more experienced orchid grower, or those with a taste for the unusual. These plants are described and their cultural requirements given. Finally, we take a look at a few of those orchids that can be grown out of doors or in an unheated alpine house and are able to cope with the rigors of a cold winter.

Left: Father-and-daughter team Brian and Sara Rittershausen have a wide knowledge of orchids, having more than fifty years of working with these wonderful plants between them.

Right: *Vanda sanderiana* was one of the early orchids to be introduced into cultivation.

VANDA SANDERIANA.

The Orchid Family

HISTORY

The question of who first cultivated orchids is one that is often asked. The answer is not as simple as it may seem. Ever since man began to live in a settled, civilized environment we may presume that he enjoyed surrounding himself with beautiful things. Although the first priority must have been to grow plants such as food crops, with civilization came more leisure time and flowers would soon play an important part. History does not tell us whether the Hanging Gardens of Babylon contained orchids, and when we look at the painted frescos in the tombs of the Valley of the Kings in Egypt there are many beautiful flowers depicted, but no orchids. We may assume, though, that if these early civilizations enjoyed all the luxuries of life then orchids would have certainly played their part.

Above: A modern miniature *Cymbidium* hybrid, descendant of the original species collected by the explorers.

The earliest recorded contact with orchids is in Chinese and Japanese manuscripts, from which we learn that they were growing dendrobiums, cymbidiums, neofinetas, and a number of other native species. The Chinese loved the *Cymbidium* species with their strong perfume and their long-lasting flowers and these were cultivated in gardens for their scent rather than their beauty. The Japanese also have a long tradition of growing *Cymbidium* species, with their love of orchids dating back three thousand years. The type of flower pot and the habit of the plant both play an important part in Japanese culture.

In Europe, the earliest recorded contact with orchids was in the pre-Roman period of the Greek Empire. The ancient Greeks believed that everything was placed on this earth for a purpose and that purpose would reveal itself if the object was studied carefully. In the case of orchids, these plants grew in great profusion all around the Mediterranean. The Greeks would identify the different species by their different uses and many were found to be suitable as herbal remedies, for curing various ailments. They also noticed that certain orchids had small, round tubers resembling a pair of testicles from which they deduced that these plants could be used as aphrodisiacs. The name "orkhis" or "orchis", the Greek for testicles, has remained with these plants ever since.

Right through until the Middle Ages, European orchids were used for many purposes and the early herbal books described their uses. It wasn't until Linnaeus, a Swedish plantsman, devised a method of classification for all plants and animals in the eighteenth century that the naming of orchids was standardized. This method, using Latin names, is still in use today and has become universally accepted.

The Explorers

When the Spanish and Portuguese began exploring new worlds, crossing the Atlantic for the first time and opening up the Americas, they also traveled down the coast of Africa and into the Indian Ocean where they explored the new lands that lay beyond. The native flora and fauna became known to the Western world, particularly the British who formed many colonies in these new lands. The explorers would return home with many treasures, among them new plants including orchids.

At the same time, the development of the greenhouse was taking place back home. Glass-making techniques were improving, allowing the manufacture of larger panes, and structures were being developed with thin wooden struts that could support these large panes and be strong enough to withstand a European winter. It was also necessary to heat these new buildings in the winter and to keep them adequately cool in hot summers, so methods of ventilating, shading, and heating had to be developed to achieve these conditions. The invention of a heating system of cast iron pipes, filled with hot water, helped to keep the houses warm in the coldest winters. Many early gardeners had never been to the tropics to experience the heat and humidity in which these plants grew so they had to experiment by trial and error, with little idea of what they were trying to achieve.

Orchids Back Home

As the interest in orchids increased, more and more plants were finding their way back to the greenhouses of England and by the early nineteenth century the modern interest in orchid growing had started. One of the most important people to encourage this interest was the Duke of Devonshire. On his estate at Chatsworth House in Derbyshire, he employed a gardener called Joseph Paxton. Paxton was a man who, encouraged by his employer's enthusiasm, was to build greenhouses of gigantic proportions,

enormous structures of steel and glass through which a coach and horses could be driven. Alas these experimental greenhouse constructions have long since gone and we are only left with pictures and the foundation stones.

The Duke's interest in orchids was tremendous, resulting in many plants being named after him. With such enthusiasm, the nurserymen of the day were quick to see a market for these new plants. They sponsored collectors to travel all over the world in search of new species and on their return, the specimens would be sent to the Royal Botanical Gardens at Kew for classification and naming. No country estate was complete without its orchid house, each one boasting a bigger and better collection than its neighbor. This interest soon spread throughout Europe and eventually reached a fever pitch almost equaling that of tulips in Holland a century or two earlier. This was the golden age of orchid collecting when the virgin jungles of the world contained unlimited supplies of plants and there was an insatiable demand for these beautiful and exotic plants back home.

Below: *Cymbidium traceyanum*, a species as popular now as it has been throughout orchid history.

Orchids in the Wild

Today, we know that orchids are one of the largest groups of flowering plants. Some 25,000–30,000 species have been identified to date. The figure varies depending on which botanical reference is used but even now when we know so much about our planet new orchids are discovered every year. Their habitats range from sea level right up to the alpine line of the highest mountains. They can be found from the snowy wastes of northern Canada and Siberia to the deserts of the Sahara. From savannahs to tropical forests, no habitat is without its successfully established orchids.

Interpreting their requirements has always been a major job for the orchid grower and is the main reason why orchid growing has developed into such a specialized branch of horticulture. The most beautiful and stunning of all the orchids are those found in the tropical rain forests and these are the plants that interest us the most, although there are many growers whose interest is in those that grow in cooler conditions. These plants can be grown in alpine greenhouses or even be planted outside in temperate areas. Tropical plants, however, have to be grown in greenhouses in temperate areas of Europe and North America, especially during the winter.

Recent History

By the dawn of the twentieth century, the interest in orchids was well established throughout Europe, and increasing on the East Coast of America. On the other side of the continent, in California, the climate was perfect for growing orchids with little or no protection.

Britain had settled down into a very orderly society with strict rules of class distinction that had existed throughout the Victorian era. This was to come to an abrupt end with the World War I, however, and the large estates in Europe declined rapidly with their labor force gone, in many cases never to return. When the war was over, a new society emerged with a totally different outlook on life and with it a fresh interest in orchids was kindled with the emphasis on the smaller, amateur grower.

By today's standards the greenhouses were still spacious and the collections large but they were small compared with those of the Victorian estates. Fewer species were being imported and the interest was concentrated more on hybrids and nursery-raised plants. This industry was based in England, raising and exporting orchids all over the world, but interest was also increasing in the emerging countries, not only in the United States but as far away as Australasia and parts of Africa. After 20 years the industry was well established and the demand for orchids was not only being met by the large nurseries in the UK, but also by those in France, Holland, Belgium, and Germany.

World War II plunged Europe into yet another conflict and many of the finest breeding stock were sent to California, Australia, New Zealand, and South Africa for safe keeping, while the nurseries in much of Europe were turned over to the production of tomatoes and other food crops for the duration of the war.

In the early 1950s, the wind of change once again introduced orchids to a different section of the population, this time keen amateurs with small collections in greenhouses in their back gardens. With this generation, the number of people growing orchids increased substantially and many orchid societies quickly formed. During the next decade, every orchid-growing country formed its own national and regional orchid societies. In North America, every major city still has at least one society, and some as many as seven. The largest orchid society, founded in the 1920s, is the American Orchid Society with members all over the world.

Japan is now at the fore of growing and breeding orchids. Some of the largest orchid shows are held there, attracting huge numbers of visitors.

ORCHID GROWING TODAY

As we enter the twenty-first century the number of purchasers is increasing, as orchids become popular houseplants. As a result, *Phalaenopsis* and *Cymbidium* are grown in vast quantities in huge nurseries devoted entirely to producing these for the potted plant market.

Most enthusiasts start with such a plant, often received as a gift, but soon their interest starts to increase. They will turn to specialty nurseries, growing only rare and unusual plants, as these tend to provide the real fascination. These nurseries can be found at the ever-increasing orchid shows, fairs, and conferences being held in every

Above: *Phalaenopsis* plants are among the most popular orchids sold for the home.

country where there is an interest in orchids.

The last two centuries have seen an enormous fascination with orchids and although this has changed as society has changed, the demand still remains. The longing to possess these beautiful flowers is still with us. So what does the future hold for orchids? Although there are still new species being discovered, the greatest advancement is now in hybridizing. With the advent of genetic engineering, colors, shapes, and sizes will be produced that have so far only been imagined. Ever increasing interest and more leisure time makes the future bright for this most ancient of hobbies.

CLASSIFICATION

As the orchid family is such a huge group of plants, it is difficult to imagine all the sections into which it could be divided. First of all we have the name orchid, the common name for all plants in the Orchidaceae family. The orchid family is divided into many sub-tribes, for example Oncidinae. These tribes are then divided into different genera, denoted by the first of the two Latin names given to all plant species, for example *Cymbidium*. The genera are then divided into different species, denoted by the second of a plant's two Latin names. For example, *floribundum* is the species name for *Cymbidium floribundum*. If these species show some natural variation, they can be further divided into varieties. As well as all these categories for naturally occurring plants, the huge amount of hybridizing that has taken place during the last 150 years has given rise to man-made names to add to the Latin ones.

As with all flowering plants, this classification is based mainly on the differences in flower shape, not necessarily on its color or on the habit of the plant. The orchid flower consists of a pattern of three outside sepals and three inside petals, known collectively as tepals. In most cases, the third petal has become exaggerated and developed differently from the rest of the flower, becoming the lip or labellum. Usually lightly hinged and capable of movement, the lip can be large and colorful, performing an ideal landing stage for visiting insects. The reproductive part of the flower, on which both the stigma and stamen are carried, is usually enclosed by the lip and is called the column.

Based on this basic pattern, it is amazing to think there are some 25,000–30,000 species all carrying a different permutation and coloring. In addition, there are over 100,000 man-made hybrids.

Fine drawings of popular new orchids of the Victorian period.

Right:
Odontoglossum crispum.

Below right:
Coelogyne cristata.

Below left:
Odontoglossum pescatorei.

TERRESTRIAL AND EPIPHYTIC ORCHIDS

Terrestrial Orchids

Just as there are many different flower shapes and colors, the plants themselves are varied too and have evolved and adapted to grow in a wide range of habitats. Orchids that grow on the ground, such as our European species, and those that grow in open grassland in the tropics, are called terrestrial orchids. Like most other plants, they usually grow with their bulbs or creeping rhizomes and roots below ground level, with only their leaves and flower spikes appearing above ground in the appropriate season.

Epiphytic Orchids

The greatest diversity of orchids can be found in the tropical rainforests that stretch across the major continents, and in fact many of the most beautiful flowers that we cultivate today have originated from this part of the world. The majority of orchids in these jungles are epiphytes, that is to say they grow on the branches and trunks of trees. They are not parasites that draw nourishment from their hosts, but simply use them for support to get away from the competition of other plants on the forest floor. Some of the very old jungles may have been undisturbed for 200,000–300,000 years and have produced an amazing evolution of fauna and flora. Very tall trees can be likened to a block of flats with different orchids living at different elevations; large, heavy plants occupying the first fork or the major limbs, and smaller, lighter plants out on the twiggy branches, with all manner of species in between.

Some orchids grow on deciduous trees, which lose their leaves in the dry season, exposing the plants to many months of bright sun. Others are much more at home in the evergreen forests living in a world of permanent twilight as the sun struggles to shine through the dappled foliage.

Epiphytic orchids have two basic growth patterns: monopodial and sympodial. Monopodial orchids have a leafy stem that grows continuously from the top. This does not necessarily mean that these plants are tall; in many the annual growth is restricted and they remain compact. The flowers develop along the stems, usually in the leaf joints. Roots can also grow along the stem as well as at the base of the plant. After the resting season is over, growth resumes at the top of the stem. Monopodial orchids include vandas, phalaenopsis, and angraecums.

Sympodial orchids have a creeping rhizome (a horizontal stem growing either at or below ground level) with new shoots growing from it each year. The flower spike often appears at the end of the stem, although it may come up from the base of the plant. Most sympodial orchids produce pseudobulbs, rather like tubers, which vary greatly in shape, size, and arrangement. These pseudobulbs help the plants to cope with both a wet and a dry

Right: Not all pseudobulbs are rounded, as many dendrobiums, with their elongated canes, show.

Below: New leaf growth on this *Coelogyne massangeana* shows where a new pseudobulb will form in the following growing season.

season each year. The plant makes a new pseudobulb each growing season during the rains, to store moisture for the plant to survive during the long periods of drought.

During the rainy season the plant has to develop as much new growth as possible. The shape of the pseudobulbs and the amount of leaves on each varies greatly from species to species. Some are completely deciduous, losing their leaves altogether during the dry season, while other orchids are lucky enough to live in evergreen forests where there is little or no dry period. These plants, through years of evolution, are continuously growing as they need no resting period; this means that they grow and flower all year round. There are also some epiphytes that have evolved with no pseudobulbs at all, just thick fleshy leaves growing in large tufts. These leaves can sustain the moisture and nourishment in the same way as the pseudobulbs.

Basic Care

Left: Watering with a rosed watering can ensures an even coverage over this tray of seedlings and creates humidity.

Above right: To give a plant a good soak, half fill a bucket with water, adding fertilizer if necessary.

Center right: Leave the plant to stand for up to 30 minutes if it has become very dry. Alternatively dunk it repeatedly in the water, immersing it for 30 seconds at a time until it is well soaked.

Below right: The water will run straight through the pot as you lift it out. Allow it to drain completely before replacing the pot on its tray.

WATERING

All living things need water and orchids are no exception. The question is how much. This depends on several factors including temperature, weather, the time of year, and the type of orchid. Plants use up more water in warm weather through transpiration and evaporation and also because it is generally warmer during summer and this is the main growing season for many orchids. While growing, orchids use up more water in producing new leaves and pseudobulbs, pumping them full of food and water ready for the winter. On dull, rainy days, even in summer, plants use less water as they do not photosynthesize much when light levels are low.

Check your orchids every few days to see how quickly the soil is drying out and get to know how heavy the pot is when just watered and how light it becomes when dry and in need of water. During the plant's growing season, try not to let it dry out too often as this can result in weak growth and the resulting pseudobulb may not flower too well. As most orchids grown in cultivation are epiphytic, avoid standing them in water as the roots will become too wet and rot. Always water your orchids from the top and let the excess water drain through; bark soil is very free draining and will let the water flow through easily which is ideal for epiphytic orchids.

In a greenhouse keep the plants on open, slatted benches to ensure the excess water runs straight through and away from the pot. With indoor orchids on window sill trays, move the plants to the sink to water them and leave them on the drain board to let the water run through before replacing them on the window sill.

As orchids are such a widespread and diverse family, they inhabit many different habitats and so require different amounts of water. For example, cattleyas like to be kept relatively dry whereas phragmipediums prefer wetter conditions. Further details on the water requirements of different plants will be discussed later in the book. Always check its water requirements when buying a plant to avoid unnecessary over- or underwatering.

Above left: When the soil has become dry it will appear paler in color and the pot will feel lighter.

Above right: Pour the water into the pot with a spouted can to prevent the crown becoming waterlogged. Continue until pools of water run from the bottom of the pot. Plants with aerial roots will also need to be misted.

FEEDING

Orchids are light feeders; in the wild they do not receive many nutrients where most of them grow, high up in the trees of the rainforests. Some amateur growers have been known to give their orchids no artificial feed at all and still grow their plants successfully. Orchids will benefit, though, from added fertilizer and those that are growing in inorganic potting mediums will rely on it. It is best for beginners to keep it simple and not worry about complex mixtures of different nutrients. Try to choose one brand of fertilizer and stick to it, at least for the whole of one season.

If you have a fairly mixed collection of orchids, different plants may be growing at different times so use the basic rule that if the plant is growing then it needs feeding and if it is not growing it does not. During the growing season, the plants will benefit from a high-nitrogen feed to boost their growth. As the season comes to an end, switch to a high-potash fertilizer which will help to ripen the pseudobulbs and encourage the flower spikes to appear.

Applying Fertilizers

Plant fertilizers tend to come in either liquid or granular form. The liquids can be unreliable because if not shaken thoroughly before each use, some of the nutrients can be left in the bottom of the bottle as sediment and not included in the solution that you give to your orchids. Granular feeds can be diluted into a solution whenever required and will not go off so easily. However, take care to keep them in an airtight container to prevent moisture getting in and turning the feed to a hard mass. The best time to apply fertilizer to your orchids is when you water the plants. Add the fertilizer to the water and pour through the soil. Use a bucket to collect the excess and reuse it during the same watering session to avoid wastage. You can also put the feed solution into a hand sprayer and apply it as a foliar feed with a fine misting over the leaves. Do not keep the mixed solution for too long as the composition may change over time, especially if left in sunlight.

As orchids do not like a strong feed, dilute the granules in double the amount of water recommended for normal houseplants and apply this on average every third watering during the growing season. This can be gradually decreased in autumn and then started again at the low rate in spring to increase to the summer program later in the year. For those orchids that may still grow during the winter, mist lightly with a weak foliar feed on bright days when the plant is going to be able to make use of the extra food.

RESTING

In some parts of the world the climate has distinct wet and dry seasons and the orchids that live there need similar treatment in cultivation. In general, when a plant is not growing it is resting. This is often when an orchid produces its flowers, drawing on the energy stored up the previous growing season. The extent of that rest varies from type to type. Some, such as pleiones, require a completely dry rest when they lose their leaves and shut down for winter. Others, such as odontoglossums, still require a little water when not in active growth to keep the pseudobulbs from shrivelling. In winter, orchids only need as much water as will keep their pseudobulbs plump. In the case of the *Coelogyne* plants that require cool temperatures, such as *C. ochracea*, an occasional dampening is all that is needed to prevent dehydration. It is quite often the cooler-growing types that have more of a definite rest; the warmer types tend to continue to grow with the extra heat available. *Phalaenopsis*, for instance, continue to grow and flower at any time of the year and so need constant attention whatever the season.

With orchids that do require a winter resting period, decrease the watering when the season's pseudobulb has been completed and can swell no more. Usually there is a bract around all or part of the pseudobulb that will turn brown when it has stopped growing. A good example of this is in *Dendrobium nobile* where the bract that attaches each leaf to the cane-like pseudobulb turns brown and papery. In this case, the cane also makes a terminal leaf at its very top to show that it is complete. Resting has finished the following spring when the next new shoot starts to appear at the base of the most recent pseudobulb; at that time watering and feeding can be gradually increased once again.

Some orchids continue to grow at a slower rate in winter than they would in summer. These need to be watered in a similar way to those that rest but need occasional watering. Give just enough to keep the new growth developing correctly and the pseudobulbs from shriveling.

HUMIDITY

In rainforests, from where many cultivated orchids come, there is usually a lot of moisture in the atmosphere and this is one reason why the orchids do so well living on trees. Without the added water in the air around them, they would quickly dry out and dehydrate. When growing orchids out of this moist environment we must try to recreate a little bit of rainforest to help them along. Spraying and misting the foliage helps to create humidity as well as cooling the leaves down in hot weather and keeping them clean and free of dust. Spraying the undersides of the leaves with water as well as the tops will discourage pests that like to hide under the leaves where they are less likely to be spotted. Red spider mite especially will thrive in a warm, dry environment.

The best time to mist orchids is in warm weather. Try to do it in the morning to allow the moisture to evaporate during the day; if too much water is left on the leaves in cold weather, or when the temperature falls at night, it can cause spotting on the leaves and may even rot new growths.

Right:
Colmanara 'Wild Cat', striking with its leopard-like spotting, is a cool-growing member of the *Odontoglossum* Alliance.

If your plants are growing in a greenhouse or conservatory, spray the floor with water every morning, a process known as "damping down," to keep humidity high without making the plants' foliage too wet. Do this more than once a day in very hot conditions to help keep the temperature down in the greenhouse. With a good, humid environment, more and more types of orchids can be grown with increased success as these are the conditions that are closest to their natural habitat.

Keeping the humidity high is more of a problem with orchids that are grown indoors. There are, though, plenty of orchids that thrive in the slightly drier atmosphere found in the home. To help increase humidity, stand the plants on trays of clay pellets which should be kept damp to gradually release their moisture into the air around the plants. Make sure that the pots aren't standing in water, however. Mist your orchids if you can from time to time, but do this when you water them at the sink to avoid ruining your furnishings.

LIGHT

Orchids are naturally shade-loving plants due to the fact that many of them originate from rainforests where there is a heavy tree canopy above them, often giving very dense shade on the forest floor. The varying amount of sunshine available at different levels of the forest means that different types of orchids need different levels of light. Little plants that may be living on the very tips of the trees' branches will be exposed to a lot more light than those growing in the lower forks of a tree, in the shade of the leaves above. And these are just the epiphytic types; there may also be terrestrial orchids growing in the ground below the trees in an even more shaded environment.

Just like other plants, though, orchids require some light to survive so we need to look at which plants we are growing to get the light levels just right.

Above: Showy vandas like this *V. 'Rothschildiana'* require good light to help them to produce regular and long-lasting flowers.

Left: Cattleyas such as this *C.* 'Louis' and 'Carla' also enjoy high light but must be shaded from the brightest rays.

Light-loving Orchids

Usually the plants with the toughest leaves are those which can take the strongest light. These include the cattleyas, laelias, and the resulting hybrids, and also orchids such as vandas, ascocentrums, rhyncostylis, and angraecums that all have thick, leathery leaves. These plants need good light because light is particularly important in the flowering of orchids. If the plant does not receive enough light then flowering may be inhibited and darker, lusher foliage may be produced instead. The plants listed above all require warm temperatures, but light is just as important for many cool-growing types.

Cymbidiums, for instance, also need a lot of light as some of these can be found growing in almost full sun in their natural habitat. A common problem with these is that they are kept in the house where there is just not enough light available so they produce a lot of leaves but no flowers.

Shade-loving Orchids

Shade-loving orchids often have softer, paler green leaves which will easily turn yellow or burn if too much light is given. A good example is *Miltoniopsis* which has soft, light green foliage and needs more shade than other orchids. Terrestrial orchids that require shade include the slipper orchids (*Phragmipedium* and *Cypripedium*) and the paphiopedilums, which often have mottled foliage to camouflage them in the dappled light on the forest floor.

In general, orchids prefer a diffused light, especially in summer when the sun is at its strongest. If the plants are placed in bright sun, the leaves can easily be scorched in a very short time. This is irreparable damage, which in severe cases can kill the plant. During the winter, the sun's rays are not strong enough to harm the plants so no extra shading is necessary; in fact you need to give the plants as much light as possible in the winter as the weather can be so dull.

Orchids in Greenhouses

If growing orchids in a greenhouse, use a simple form of artificial shading to control the levels of light. Apply the first layer of shading at the beginning of spring. This can be either shade netting or shading paint, or a combination of the two. The position of your greenhouse will dictate how much shading you need; for example, some greenhouses are close to deciduous trees which provide shade in summer so less artificial shade would be needed. As the spring and summer go on you can increase the shade with a second layer if required, eventually aiming to block out 50 percent of the light in the brightest summer months. By early autumn you may wish to remove some of the shading, to be reapplied the following spring. The aim is to achieve good light, but not bright direct sunshine; if you can stand in the greenhouse and look up at the shaded roof without squinting, then the level is just right.

Above right: Popular house plants such as *Phalaenopsis* 'Cool Breeze' will grow well in indirect sun all year round.

Below right: *Miltoniopsis*, such as this *M.* 'Eureka', are naturally shade-loving orchids.

Below: Miniature *Phalaenopsis*, such as this primary hybrid between *P. venosa* and *P. violacea*, need good light in order to flower well but must be shaded from the direct summer sun.

Indoor Orchids

If growing orchids in the home, shade may need to be provided, particularly if they are growing in a bright, south-facing window. A net curtain may be enough to shade them from the sun; if not, move them back into the room a little on the brightest days. Alternatively, place a piece of greenhouse shade netting between the plants and the window to create a shaded environment. You could also move your orchids to a north-facing window in summer, moving them back to the south-facing position for the winter. As well as lowering light levels, protecting plants from the sun will also lower the temperature, helping to keep the plants cooler on hot days.

VENTILATION

Ventilation is also important in keeping orchids cool. Ventilators or windows in a greenhouse or conservatory that can be opened on hot days will help keep temperatures down. Automated ventilation systems are a good idea, as a greenhouse that is shut up on a hot day can rise to over 105° F (40° C). Under these conditions, plants will suffer and may never recover.

Take into consideration the ventilators when putting on your shading, as they may have to open through the netting. If you are worried about insects such as bumble bees entering the greenhouse when the ventilators or doors are left open, attach a piece of shade netting across the openings to let the air flow through but keep out the insects that might shorten the life of your flowers.

In the home, ventilation is important too. It will help to open windows from time to time, as the plants will benefit from air movement as long as they are not in cold drafts.

Left: Cymbidiums are often grown for cut flowers in large greenhouses devoted to just one variety. Good ventilation is used to keep the blooms cool, in order to prolong their life when cut.

Right above: *Cattleya trianaei* requires an intermediate temperature range, as do all *Cattleya* Alliance members.

Right: Vandas are generally hot-growing as many of the species originate from the tropics.

Far right: *Odontoglossum* 'Geyser Gold' is a cool-growing hybrid, needing a drop in temperature in winter in order to bloom well.

TEMPERATURE

Orchids tend to be grouped according to the temperature range that they require to grow successfully. There are three main groups: cool, intermediate, and warm.

Minimum Temperatures

The cool-growing orchids tend to originate from high altitudes in mountain ranges such as the Himalayas and Andes where night-time temperatures can drop as low as 40° F (5° C). It is usually in the dry season that the temperature falls this low, so the plants are often resting and can cope with the cold when combined with dryness. Pleiones are a good example, as they come from high in the Himalayas and enjoy a cold, dry rest when they have lost their season's growth of leaves.

Although they need a severe drop in temperature, orchids do not generally benefit from being exposed to frost as this can cause damage and may kill the plant. Most of the cool-growing orchids, however, do not want a drop quite as low as 40° F (5° C). For the most popular genera, such as *Cymbidium*, *Odontoglossum*, and *Dendrobium*, a minimum of 50° F (10° C) is adequate. The figure that is quoted is usually the minimum below which it should not drop on the coldest winter night. This gives an indication as to how much artificial heat you need to provide in winter, which will be your biggest expense.

Intermediate types require to be a few degrees warmer, the minimum winter temperature being around 55° F (12° C) for *Miltoniopsis* and *Cattleya*, for example. The warm-growing orchids need to be kept above 60° F (15° C) to ensure they are growing at their best. *Phalaenopsis* and *Paphiopedilum* are typical of this group. If orchids are allowed to drop to below their required minimum temperature on a regular basis or are given a sudden, sharp drop, it can be very detrimental to the plant. Equally, if cool-growing orchids are kept consistently too warm, they will either not grow as well as they should or they will grow too well and produce new leaves rather than flowers.

Maximum Temperatures

Maximum temperatures are also important. In summer, the temperature should not rise above 75° F (24° C) for cool-growing orchids and 85° F (28° C) for the warm-growing plants. In very hot weather, try to keep the temperature down as much as possible by using misting, shading, and ventilation.

In warm weather during the summer months, there should be no need for artificial heating, especially for cool-growing plants. If night-time temperatures are favorable then even warm-growing orchids can be raised without extra heat.

To keep a constant check on the temperature around the orchids, use a maximum/minimum thermometer, which will tell you how low the temperature drops during the night or how high it rises during the day.

Temperature Fluctuation

Temperature fluctuation is a natural occurrence: days are warmer than nights and winter is cooler than summer. These daily and seasonal changes are important to keep the orchids on their correct growing and flowering cycles. A drop in temperature during winter, especially at night, tells cool-growing orchids that the growing season is ending and it is time to start slowing down and producing flowers. Cymbidiums

are a good example of this. If the plants are kept warm during winter, they are tricked into believing it is still summer and will not flower while on their summer cycle. Light levels also contribute to this but it is the temperature that is most important.

Even warm-growing types can be kept too warm and will continue to grow without producing blooms. If your *Phalaenopsis* is a little shy to flower, move the plant to a position where the temperature is just a few degrees cooler and hopefully, within a few weeks, a flower spike should appear.

Extremes of Temperature

Although orchids need fluctuation, extremes in temperature are not welcome. The appearance of a plant that has been either frozen or cooked is very similar. The cells in the leaves have been put under severe stress and broken down. A secondary bacterial infection quickly sets in, creating a black patch on the leaves that spreads swiftly over the surface of

the foliage. This can then spread to the rest of the plant and will easily kill it in severe circumstances. These symptoms are commonly seen when winter heating breaks down on a cold night, or when no ventilation is provided on a hot summer's day. In extreme cases the plant

may not survive but in mild cases, remove the worst affected leaves or parts of the plant and make sure that it is pampered for a time to enable it to make a full recovery.

GREENHOUSE CULTURE

To enable the most suitable environment to be created for your orchids, the best place to keep them is a greenhouse. By devoting the whole area to orchids, you can concentrate on getting the conditions just right.

If you are starting from scratch then there are many different greenhouse designs from which to choose; select whichever one best suits the position and aesthetics of your home. Consider the position of the greenhouse carefully. If the structure is built under deciduous trees they will provide the necessary shade in summer, but evergreen trees will also block the light during the dull months of the year when it is needed. Having the greenhouse in an open position makes it easier to control the light levels as you can apply and remove shading at different times of the year as required. For this you can use shade netting attached to the roof or apply shading paint to the glass, or a combination of the two methods. Remember, though, that a greenhouse in an exposed position will not be sheltered from the wind, which can cause extensive damage.

Whether you choose a wooden or a metal-framed greenhouse does not really matter. Wooden greenhouses do tend to dry out more slowly than the metal ones, so you may want to bear this in mind. Traditionally all greenhouses were made of glass sheets; this is still the most popular and cheapest way of providing a strong shell but the glass can break, especially in windy weather. There is now an alternative which, although more expensive initially, is an extremely economical method of roofing your greenhouse.

This is polycarbonate sheeting and can be obtained in many different forms. It comprises two or three layers of rigid plastic sheet, joined by thin walls that hold the sheets apart, forming pockets of air. This is excellent insulation that helps to keep warmth inside the greenhouse in cold weather. The polycarbonate can also be tinted to give permanent shade.

If your greenhouse is glass then extra insulation can be created by lining the house with thick bubble-plastic sheeting. This also helps to block any drafts. Regular inspections should be made to close any gaps that form between the panes of glass.

Ventilation

If it is a new greenhouse you are building for your orchids or an existing one being converted to an orchid-friendly house, the basic needs are the same. Light and insulation have already been mentioned but ventilation is also very important. On warm days, even with shade the temperature of the house can rise rapidly to a very high point without adequate ventilation. There are automated systems, governed by a thermostat, which can be installed to open ventilators when the temperature reaches a certain point. However, the ventilators may have to be opened and closed by hand and this can be a problem if you are away for any length of time during unpredictable weather. Orchids can literally cook if left in an unventilated greenhouse in hot weather when the temperature can rise above 100° F (38° C). When setting up your greenhouse make sure that there are ventilators in both the roof and the sides of the house. You can also leave the doors open if you are around during the day, to provide extra air movement.

Positioning Plants

Strong, movable staging is essential for your orchids and can be set at whatever height suits you and the plants. Larger plants can be positioned lower to the ground, for example, and smaller ones higher up. The staging should be made of open slats or mesh to enable water to drain away freely from the bases of the pots. To increase the available space in your house, think of it in three dimensions, using the space above the staging to hang orchids in baskets or hanging pots. Those that prefer more light will enjoy being higher up and will create a bit of shade for the ones underneath. Take care not to pack your house too full though, as this can cut out the light reaching the plants and they may not grow or flower as well.

You may also like to make use of the walls by growing plants mounted on pieces of cork bark. They can be suspended on mesh fixed to the sides of the greenhouse where they can be regularly sprayed to keep them moist.

Companion Plants

The space underneath the benches can be a little dark for most orchids but is ideal for many of the companion plants that enjoy a shady, humid spot, such as ferns, bromeliads, and other foliage plants. Either keep these in pots or plant them into the ground under the benches. Check these plants regularly as they can harbor pests that can spread on to your orchids if left to thrive undisturbed.

The companion plants also have an important role in helping to increase the humidity in the greenhouse. Rainforest plants do not live alone and will grow better in the company of other plants.

Humidity

Humidity is easy to create in a greenhouse by damping down the floor with water each morning, especially in hot weather. In cooler or dull weather, spraying is not so essential and can be damaging to flowers and sometimes even the plants themselves if the water collects on the plants' foliage. Together with spraying over the floor, you can also apply a light misting to the orchids' leaves. As well as raising humidity, this helps to keep them free of dust and pests; remember to mist the undersides of the leaves too.

Certain orchids such as vandas, which grow without any soil around their roots, rely on regular misting to provide them with the moisture that they need to prevent dehydration.

Watering

Misting can be done on a daily basis but this may not provide enough water for many orchids. They also need to be given water at their roots and this is easily done when they are growing in a greenhouse. For greater efficiency, use a watering lance attached to a hose that is long enough to reach all the plants without the need to continually refill a watering can. The lance can be used

Above: *Dendrochilum glumaceum* provides a beautiful show in the winter with its feathery sprays of very strongly scented flowers.

with a variety of roses and misting heads to suit most needs. If you cannot arrange a main water supply in your greenhouse, set up a water tank inside which can be filled regularly. This means the water will be at a warmer temperature to use in the winter when outside taps and pipes can freeze. Try to fill the tank with rainwater if possible.

Heating

Heating is, of course, an important factor in a greenhouse and the temperature you require will depend on which orchids you are growing. If you are growing those that require warmer temperatures, you will obviously need to heat the house more often so the most efficient method is preferable. There are many different forms of heating equipment fueled by gas, electricity and oil. It is important that there is plenty of ventilation with gas-fueled heating, as the fumes can be harmful to the plants as well as the growers if allowed to build up. If you are not able to connect to a gas main, a kerosene heater will work well. Electric fan heaters are effective at circulating the heat around the greenhouse, but can create a rather dry atmosphere so regular spraying may be necessary to keep up the humidity. Oil heaters are not as cost-effective but can be used as a back-up system in case of emergency.

Potting Orchids

SOILS

Over the years of orchid cultivation there have been many, many different ideas on what to grow the orchids in. Still today there is a wide range of different soils from which to choose, both those that can be bought ready-mixed and those that can be mixed at home from a variety of ingredients. For the beginner this can be a little confusing so it is best to keep it simple.

As many of the orchids that we grow are epiphytic in the wild, it is logical to use an open, free-draining soil. High up on the trees in the rainforests, orchids cling to branches without much around their roots apart from the leaf litter and moss that collects there. The rain washes down the branches over the roots of the orchids and continues to drain away from the plants to the forest floor. These are the conditions that we should try to recreate in the orchid pot. The type of soil that most resembles these natural growing conditions is made up of bark chippings and so bark-based mixes are used for most orchids.

There are several different grades of bark that can be used for different types or sizes of orchids. The finest grade contains pieces of bark that are, on average, ¼ in. (5 mm) across and this is ideal for very young orchid seedlings or mature miniature orchids that have a fine root system. As the young plants mature and are moved into larger pots they can be potted into a coarser grade of bark; each piece in this grade measures around 1 in. (2 cm). Certain types of orchid prefer an even coarser mix, such as cattleyas which like to be kept relatively dry; bark with quite large chunks will not hold the water for as long as the finer grades.

Try to buy bark chippings that have been produced especially for orchids. The bark that is sold for mulching flower beds in the garden can be very rough and contains a lot of white sap wood pieces which are not easy to use in a pot and do not hold moisture well. An even grade with bark pieces of a similar size is the best. The most commonly used barks are pine and fir, which are stripped in timber production. Redwood barks are also available and are of a higher quality, so tend to be a little more expensive.

There are many additives that can be used in conjunction with the bark to aid either moisture retention or drainage. Moss peat or a peat substitute will help to prevent the soil drying out, by holding water. This is good for those orchids that prefer to be relatively moist, such as the terrestrial paphiopedilums and pleiones. It is also common to add perlite or the larger perlag into a peat and bark mix as this helps with the drainage, preventing the soil from becoming too wet. These are types of porous volcanic rock that have been reduced to very small granules. A mixture of peat, fine grade bark, and perlite, for instance, is ideal for young seedlings.

Before bark soils were so easily available, the most common potting mixes were made from sphagnum moss and osmunda fern fiber. This fibrous root system of the osmunda fern is not so easily obtainable now but can still be used; bear in mind, however, that it dries out easily. Sphagnum moss is still regularly used; it is usually purchased in dried and compacted form, which is rehydrated with water. This will not bring it back to

nutrients that the plant requires have to be given via the water.

This method of growing has proved to be very successful for some orchids, and growers are increasingly using it for odontoglossums, phragmipediums, and miltoniopsis to name but a few. Although the plants seem to grow well in this alien mixture, a certain amount of experience and care is needed. The fertilizing regime should be carefully worked out and adhered to, ensuring the plants are getting all they need to grow and flower well. Also, it is advisable to wear gloves when handling the substance as the minute glass fibers that make up the grey, woolly substance can easily get under the skin and cause irritation. Moisten the rockwool before use and, for extra protection, wear a facemask to prevent inhalation of the irritating dust.

Another man-made potting substance is horticultural foam. This is chopped into small chunks, which can be mixed into a peat or bark mix or even used alone. If used alone, it is treated much the same as rockwool, with the plants needing careful feeding as it contains no organic components.

life, but the moss helps by holding moisture around the orchids' roots and is especially good for potting sickly plants to aid recovery.

Another possible addition to soil mixes, which is becoming increasingly popular, is chunks of coconut fiber. This performs a similar role to the bark in holding some moisture while still draining freely.

Inorganic Potting Mixes

In recent years there has been an increasing trend towards inorganic potting media. These are man-made substances that contain no natural ingredients. The most popular is rockwool, which is made from manufactured glass fibers similar to the substance that is used in insulation. It is usually mixed with perlite, which is added for drainage, and is very good at holding moisture around the roots. Rockwool has to be kept moist at all times for the plants to thrive; this growing method is based on hydroponics—growing plants in water. Due to the fact that the medium is entirely inorganic, all the

Left: Bags of orchid bark potting soil are generally packed dry to make the contents last longer although there will always be some condensation showing.

Above: A bark-based soil is usually the most suitable because it is free-draining.

Right: Coconut fiber makes a good substance for mounting orchids onto cork bark as it gives the roots a good network to adhere to.

REPOTTING

Sympodial orchids that grow new pseudobulbs each season, connected by an advancing rhizome, will inevitably outgrow their pot in time. This is the time for the plant to be repotted to give more room for the next year's growth. Plants do not usually become root-bound; although there are orchids that produce a large amount of roots, the problem is more often a lack of space in the top of the pot for the pseudobulbs. The frequency of repotting depends on how well a plant has been growing and this varies from type to type. Some orchids make abundant new growths each year and outgrow their pot quite easily whereas others may only make one new pseudobulb a year and take several years to fill the pot. If the plant has been grown particularly well and is hanging out over the side of the container, then it may need to be put into a new pot which is several sizes larger than the original.

Organic soils such as bark can start to break down after a number of years, so as well as giving the plant more room, repotting is an ideal opportunity to refresh the potting medium. Inorganic soils such as rockwool will not break down so this does not need to be completely cleaned out from the roots. If you are transferring the plant from one type of soil to another, it is a good idea to clean out all the previous soil as mixing the two can cause problems when the plant is watered.

Repotting should preferably be carried out in the spring or when the plant is just starting its new growth. It is then that the new roots are produced which can grow straight down into the new soil, causing minimum disturbance to the plant.

The first step is obviously to remove the plant from its original pot. This is not always as easy as it sounds. Cymbidiums, for instance, can make a very solid mass of roots that make even a plastic pot very difficult to remove. This may have to be done by cutting the pot away with a sharp knife.

Trimming the Roots

When you remove the plant from the pot, the roots you see should look healthy and be white with perhaps some green or yellow growing tips to them. If too many of the roots are brown and soft, wet even, then the plant has been kept too wet and the roots have started to rot. It is natural for the plant to lose some of its old roots as new ones are produced each year and some of these can be trimmed back to a length of 1–2 in. (3–5 cm), depending on the size of the plant. Use a sharp pair of pruning shears or scissors for this job and make sure that they have been sterilized between plants by dipping them in rubbing alcohol to avoid any contamination that may occur. Try to avoid damaging any new and active roots when you do this. It is, however, often unavoidable and if they do break they will easily grow back. By pruning back the root ball we are encouraging the plant to make new roots as well as making room in the pot for them. Do not be afraid to be a little brutal but do not cut the roots too short; leave enough to be a strong anchor in the new pot. When you have trimmed the roots, clean out the old soil either directly into a rubbish bin or on to a piece of newspaper that can be disposed of easily before starting to pot with fresh soil.

Tidying the Top Growth

This is also a good time to tidy the plant a little. When old leaves die they often leave behind a bract around the pseudobulb, which dies and turns brown. These can be removed along with any old pseudobulbs that have died. Pseudobulbs do not live forever and although they are a vital food store, they are eventually spent. If they have turned brown and shriveled up, then cut through the rhizome that connects them to the live parts of the plant and discard them. If there are leafless pseudobulbs at the back of the orchid that are still plump and green, leave these alone as they are still acting as stores for food and water. There can sometimes be an excess of these leafless back bulbs and they can be removed and used for propagation; this will be looked at in more detail later on (see page 45).

Left above: Remove the plant, here a cymbidium, from its pot, clean out the old soil and trim back the root ball with a sharp pair of pruning shears.

Left: Root pruning does not hurt the plant. In fact it stimulates new growth and ensures there is room in the new pot to produce more roots.

Above: Repot orchids, like this bulbophyllum, when the new growth is quite young as this is when new roots are made and least disturbance is caused.

Choosing a Pot

Now the orchid has been tidied, trimmed, and cleaned, the next stage is to find a new pot for it. Every plant is different so it is best to try the plant in several different pots to see which one looks best. Avoid putting the plant in a pot that is too big for it, thinking that it will need repotting less often. This does not work as invariably the soil ends up being too wet, causing problems to arise. Do not put the plant in too small a pot either; it needs enough room to be able to grow for another couple of years before it fills the pot once again. Generally a new pot just a little larger than the original will be sufficient. Plastic pots are more popular now as they are lighter and less easy to break, but clay pots still have a more attractive appearance and are perfectly acceptable for orchids. Whichever type you use, make sure it has plenty of drainage holes in the base.

Right:
1 Use polystyrene chips or pebbles for drainage.

2 Place the plant in the pot with space for growth. Do not bury it or set it too high.

3 Fill in with bark soil. Firm this down with your thumbs or a potting stick. Do not push on the plant itself.

4 The new shoot sits on the soil surface, just below the rim of the pot.

Below: A step up of about two pot sizes is usually adequate.

Repotting

Once you have chosen a pot, you can repot the plant. You may wish to use some drainage material in the base. Pebbles serve well but can make the pot unnecessarily heavy. A better, lighter alternative is polystyrene chips. They will not break down but will keep a layer of air in the base of the pot. You may have found some of these in the base when you removed the plant from its original pot. A single layer of chips is adequate.

Next place a layer of the moistened potting mixture on top of them and place the plant on top of this. Hold the plant in position with the older pseudobulbs towards one edge of the pot and a space in front of the new shoots for them to fill. The roots should be sitting on the layer of soil with the shoots just below the rim of the pot. While holding the plant still with one hand, use the other hand to fill the spaces in the pot with more soil. Continue to add soil, firming it down until the plant seems to be stable enough for you to let go of it. Then, using your thumbs or a potting stick, firm the soil down so the plant is held well in place. Bark soils are fairly springy and will push down easily. Looser mixes such as rockwool and perlite do not need to be compressed to such an extent. Continue to fill the pot with more soil until the level is just below the rim of the pot. If it is too full, the soil will wash out over the sides of the pot during watering.

Once you have finished, the plant should be firm in its pot and not liable to fall out or wobble; a plant that is not firm will not be able to root easily. Remember to replace the name label in the pot and make a note of the date of repotting, if you wish.

BASKETS

Many orchids lend themselves to growing in hanging baskets and these are available in many differing shapes, sizes and materials. Orchids will really grow in any sort of container as long as it has plenty of drainage holes. Wire or plastic baskets, as used in the garden, are good but they can sometimes be a little open, letting soil wash out every time the plant is watered. To overcome this, place a layer of plastic netting in the base of the basket before the orchid is potted into it. Greenhouse shade netting is ideal as it will not break down easily. Plastic net pots are also very good, especially for smaller plants; aquatic plant baskets are perfect examples. Orchids such as gongoras produce a great many aerial roots so a net pot will allow these to grow out into the air with ease. They also produce pendent flower spikes that hang over the side of the container or even grow downwards through the holes, so a hanging situation is essential. *Coelogyne massangeana* is another pendent bloomer, the spikes reaching up to 24 in. (60 cm) in length, so it looks at its best when the beautiful tresses of yellow flowers are allowed to hang below a basket.

Right: Many orchids grow well in wooden slatted baskets, often growing out the side, in-between the slats, like this *Stanhopea.*

Far right:
1 The new shoot of this *Coelogyne massangeana* is near the edge of the pot without enough room to grow into a new pseudobulb.

2 If a plant is very root bound, apply pressure to the side of the pot to release the root ball.

3 Clean out the old soil and any old crocks onto some newspaper so they can be disposed of easily.

4 Many types of decorative baskets, such as this white framed one with a coconut fiber lining, are available.

5 Choose a basket large enough to allow your orchid to grow for another 2–3 years. Position the plant so there is space around the new shoots.

6 Fill in with bark soil around the plant.

7 Push the soil down firmly around only the edge of the container in order to avoid damaging the plant.

8 Don't forget to replace the name label and mark when you repotted the plant.

9 Water the basket thoroughly before hanging it in your greenhouse or conservatory.

Without a basket the *Stanhopea* would not be able to bloom properly. The flower spike is sent down through the soil and out of the side or the base of the basket. If there are no holes the spike will eventually abort when it cannot find a way out. The most popular type of basket for stanhopeas and most other orchids is a

wooden slatted basket. These are used extensively in the Far East for keeping vandas and other orchids where little or no soil is used around the roots. This will only work if there is a very high level of humidity and the plant will be able to take in all the moisture that it needs directly through its roots. If insufficient moisture is provided, the orchid will start to dehydrate. Therefore, in conditions that are not as humid as the tropics it is better to add soil to the wooden baskets.

Transferring an orchid from a pot into a basket is no more difficult than simple repotting. Choose a basket large enough so that the plant will be able to grow in it for at least two years, but take care not to overpot into too large a container. Many orchids suited to baskets, bulbophyllums for example, will remain in the same container for years as they love to grow over the sides and eventually completely envelop the whole thing if left alone. Line the inside of the basket with netting to prevent the soil being washed out, and pot as normal with a fairly open, coarse bark soil. There is good drainage in a basket so there is no need to add drainage material in the bottom.

By using hanging baskets in your greenhouse or conservatory, you are making use of the whole space, right up to the roof. The orchids that you hang up should be those that enjoy the extra light that they will receive nearer the roof. You may find that they also dry out more quickly due to the increased airflow around the root system, so make certain that the plants are getting enough water in warm weather.

MOUNTING ON BARK

As we have already seen, many orchids grow as epiphytes on rainforest trees in the wild. We too can grow orchids in this way by mounting them on to pieces of cork bark or decorative wood. Certain plants are well suited to being mounted in this way, especially those with a creeping rhizome that will allow the plant to grow across the surface very easily. If the plant also produces a lot of aerial roots then it will adapt well to being transferred to a bark mount. Orchids growing in this way need regular spraying and watering, as they will dry out much more quickly than those growing in pots where their roots are enclosed in moist soil. It is best to grow bark-mounted orchids in a greenhouse or conservatory where they can be sprayed every day.

Transfer a pot-grown plant to a bark mount when the plant is just beginning to make new growth, as this is when the new roots will start to appear. Do not move the plant if it is in flower or bud. Find a piece of cork bark or wood that is slightly longer than the plant to give it enough room to grow for several years before it needs to be moved. For the plant to be able to root well, the bark surface should be quite rough; the roots will grow into nooks and crannies. This is why the bark of cork oak is so popular and effective, though many other types of bark and wood are suitable. Avoid beach driftwood, however, unless it has been soaked thoroughly to remove the sea salt.

Before starting to fix your plant on to the mount, decide which way up it is going to hang and make a hole in one end of the mount with a bradawl, through which you can feed a piece of wire. Bend the wire into a hook.

Remove the plant from its pot and clean off the roots, removing all the old soil. Trim back some of the older roots to about 1–2 in. (3–5 cm), taking care not to damage any new roots.

To give the roots something to grow into and help keep moisture around them, make a pad of either sphagnum moss or coconut fiber, or a mixture of the two. This should be wrapped around the roots and placed as a cushion between the plant and the mount when positioning the orchid in its correct place on the surface. While holding the plant in place, pass a length of plastic-coated wire over the rhizome between the pseudobulbs, and twist the ends together to fasten at the back or side of the bark. Tighten the wire just enough to hold the plant firm; be careful not to let it cut into the flesh of the rhizome. Avoid putting the wire across the new growth as it can easily be damaged. Several ties may be necessary depending on the size of the plant. Your orchid should now be given a thorough watering and it is especially important that this is done regularly at first to encourage new root growth.

Many orchids can be grown successfully in this way and, for the greatest effect, try making an epiphyte tree by mounting several orchids and bromeliads on an old tree branch.

Far right:
1 This *Miltonia spectabilis* has outgrown its pot, it would be happier trained onto some cork bark.

2 Cut the piece growing over the side away from the main plant, making sure it has no fewer than four pseudobulbs.

3 At this length it will have enough aerial roots to establish itself onto the bark.

4 Hold the plant onto a pad of coconut fiber or sphagnum moss.

5 Place the plant onto the cork with the mat in-between. Leave room for the new growth.

6 Pass a piece of plastic-coated wire between two of the pseudo-bulbs and fasten it at the back by twisting it tight.

7 Larger plants may need several ties.

8 The plant now needs watering thoroughly.

9 Thread a hook through the hole you made in the bark earlier. Hang the orchid in a place where it can get high humidity and is in easy reach so that you can spray it every day.

Right: In their natural rainforest habitat, many epiphytic orchids can be found growing on trees, as seen here in Costa Rica.

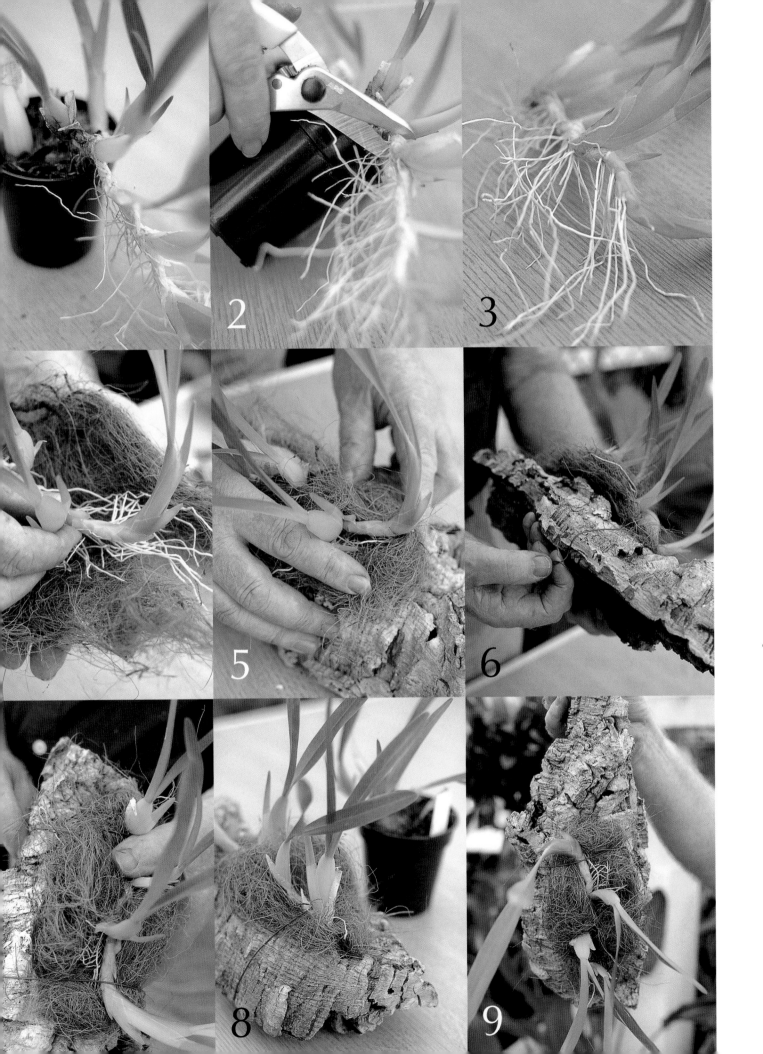

Propagation

DIVIDING ORCHIDS

While the natural method of propagating orchids, by seed, is a little beyond the reach of most amateur growers, dividing plants is a more accessible method of increasing stock. Sympodial orchids that grow with pseudobulbs are the easiest to divide. Each of the pseudobulbs is connected to the others by a thick rhizome which can either be very short, making the pseudobulbs close together, or longer giving the plant a creeping habit. If each season the leading, or newest, pseudobulb only makes one new growth, then it is going to be many years before the plant can be divided, if at all. However, if the plant makes two or more new growths from the leading pseudobulb each year then they will increase in number quickly, making a larger plant with many leading growths. It is this type of orchid that can be most easily divided into two or more plants, depending on the size.

Right: Cut through the connecting rhizome, between the pseudobulbs, and pull the two sections apart. The root ball will probably have to be cut through too.

Left: Each division should comprise of no fewer than 4 to 5 pseudobulbs, each with at least one new growth.

Dividing a Cymbidium

One of the most popular types of orchid that amateur growers want to divide is the *Cymbidium*. These plants can grow quite large and the standard varieties can take over a small space within a few years. Cymbidiums will regularly make multiple new shoots so the number of pseudobulbs can increase quickly. When dividing a plant, take into consideration the number of pseudobulbs. The resulting divisions should consist of not less than four or five pseudobulbs, each with at least one new growth.

Removing the Plant from its Pot

If the plant is very pot-bound and overdue for repotting and dividing, it may take some effort to release it from the pot. If it proves too much of a challenge, then you may have to cut off the pot, or smash it if it is terracotta. When the plant has been removed, it may be immediately apparent where it can be divided; the plant may even fall into several pieces once out of the pot. More likely, though, the pseudobulbs and roots will be tightly packed together and it may take some degree of maneuvering to separate the pseudobulbs.

Dividing the Plant

As previously mentioned, each section should end up with at least one new growth plus four or five recently made pseudobulbs. As the pseudobulbs age they tend to gradually lose their leaves which leave a brown, papery bract. These can become quite unsightly so it is best to remove them as they appear, or, alternatively, at the time of potting, which is an excellent opportunity to tidy the plant. If the pseudobulbs have become shriveled and dried up or perhaps rotten and wet inside, then remove them. It is at the point where an old pseudobulb has died that the plant may be divided as an obvious gap has been formed between two plants.

If there are no old pseudobulbs to remove then a different dividing point must be found. This should be between two older pseudobulbs that are positioned several places back in the line from the new shoot. Cut through the woody rhizome that connects the pseudobulbs with a sharp and sterile knife. This will make it easier to part the two halves of the plant and roots too can be cut through where they are interwoven. It may seem brutal to be slicing through the plant, but if done correctly, and at the correct time of year (spring for cymbidiums and most other orchids), then there should be no harm done and in fact the plant will probably benefit from it. Pot up the separate divisions as described on page 38 and treat as normal.

Back-bulb Propagation

Occasionally, cymbidiums have an excess of older pseudobulbs that are still green, firm and have dormant eyes at their base, and which have not rotted away through old age. If these pseudobulbs are removed from the parent plant and potted up separately, or in a community pot together if there are several, there is a good chance that they will, in turn, start to grow a new shoot. This method is called back-bulb propagation and is a popular way to propagate cymbidiums. Before meristemming

methods of cloning were introduced (see page 46), this was the only way of multiplying a stock of a special variety and rare back-bulbs of awarded clones fetched high prices. Pot the back-bulbs into a mix of bark and peat in a fairly small pot until they are established. Keep them warm and humid, either in a propagator or in a plastic bag, tied at the top to maintain humidity. Water occasionally, keeping the soil just moist. This should encourage the growth of any eyes that are lying dormant waiting to grow. The energy and food that is stored up in the pseudobulb will help to make a new shoot that will probably be rather

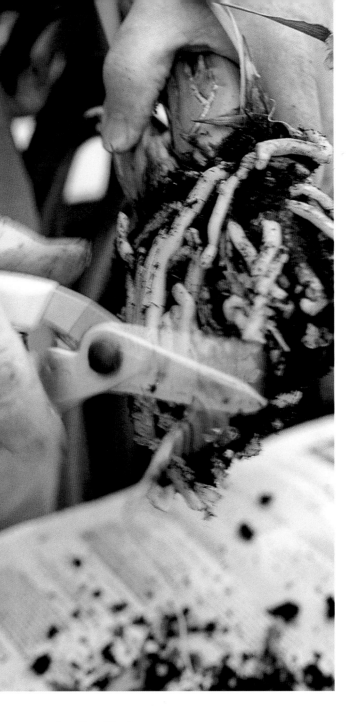

Above: Clean out as much of the old soil as possible and trim back any dead roots. Newer roots can also be trimmed, as this encourages new ones to be produced. Ensure the roots that remain are at least 2¼–4 in. (6–10cm) in length to help anchor the plant in the new pot.

weak at first. The first new pseudobulb that it makes will be small but with each year's new growth, the size of the pseudobulb should increase with correct culture until eventually the plant is large enough to flower. This process can take up to five years so a little patience is needed.

Dividing other Orchids

Most sympodial orchids can be split in the same way as cymbidiums, although some may take longer to reach a dividable size. Some too will readily grow from back-bulbs, including lycastes, coelogynes, brassias, and encyclias. Dendrobiums have many dormant eyes present all along the length of their elongated, cane-like pseudobulbs. These are really designed to produce flowers but they can be encouraged to produced offshoots called "keikis." Sometimes the keikis are not wanted as they are readily produced instead of flower buds if the plant has inadvertently been kept too warm or wet during its winter resting period. If, however, you want to encourage these growths, then those are the conditions in which to keep the plant to obtain them. Another way is to remove an old but still green cane from the parent plant and lay this in a tray of damp sphagnum moss and it keep regularly sprayed. *Dendrobium nobile* and its hybrids are particularly successful. Cut the cane into sections between the eyes and dip the cut ends into sulfur to prevent any infection getting into the tissue. The eyes on the canes will begin to grow into young plants which can be potted up individually when they have formed their own root system. Other orchids that produce keikis include thunias, calanthes, and pleiones. Phalaenopsis are also known to make keikis from the eyes along their flower stems.

Dividing Cattleyas

Members of the *Cattleya* group can often be divided and propagated while still in their pots. If a plant has a lot of older pseudobulbs in the pot and the newer section at the front is growing over the side of the container, as cattleyas have a habit of doing, the rhizome can be cut between two of the older pseudobulbs towards the back of the plant. If there are dormant eyes on the old pseudobulbs, then one or more of these should then start to grow and root into the existing pot. When this section is established, the whole plant can be repotted and the two sections separated. Cattleyas respond well to this treatment and it is an ideal way to increase your collection.

TISSUE CULTURE

Growing from seed is obviously the way that orchids reproduce themselves in the wild and a way we can produce new and exciting hybrids in cultivation, as there is always some variation in the offspring. But if there is one particularly fine orchid that a commercial grower wishes to mass-produce, with all the offspring identical to the parent plant, then how can this be done? The answer is meristem culture.

Orchids with pseudobulbs have several eyes from which the new shoots or flower spikes can grow. At the center of these eyes, under several layers of protective sheaths, is the meristem cell from which the new leaf or spike forms. If this meristem is removed under sterile conditions, it can then be grown on to produce a new green protocorm. If the protocorm is placed in a nourishing liquid gel and is constantly rotated to keep it moving, it will continue to grow into a larger ball of cells and will not produce leaves or roots. The protocorm is then repeatedly divided over time to produce more and more protocorms. These are then transferred to a solid gel where they will begin to produce leaves and roots.

The resulting group of plants will be genetically identical to the original plant from which the tissue was extracted and will all produce nearly identical flowers. This breakthrough in orchid propagation has enabled the mass production of thousands of different orchids, even those that have won coveted awards, improving the quality of plants and making them cheaper and more widely available to orchid enthusiasts the world over.

This method of production is most commonly performed with genera such as *Cymbidium*, the *Odontoglossum* group, the *Cattleya* group, *Miltoniopsis,* and *Dendrobium.* In addition, similar techniques are used with vandas in which the leaf tip is taken and used for propagation. Most recently, mass production of *Phalaenopsis* has really taken off with the perfection of a stem propagation technique. The flower stem of a phalaenopsis has several eyes along its length and these can be removed and placed on a special gel containing growth hormones, which encourage the eye to form a new plant instead of a flower spike. This technique has revolutionized the production of these orchids, which are now the most popular orchid pot plants in the world.

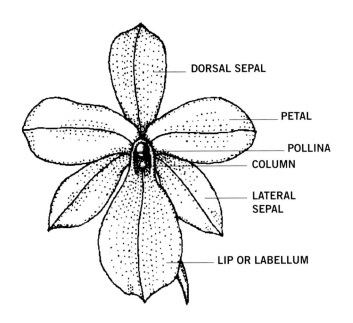

DORSAL SEPAL

PETAL

POLLINA

COLUMN

LATERAL
SEPAL

LIP OR LABELLUM

POLLINATION

Within the extremely large and diverse family of orchids, there are an infinite number of different flower shapes, sizes, styles, colors, and patterns. To the uninitiated it can seem like a wondrous maze of orchids and it is difficult to believe that they are all related to one another, especially with all the different plant structures and sizes too. There is one factor, though, that is the same for all orchids and that is the flower structure.

The Structure of an Orchid Flower

As we have already seen, firstly there are the three sepals which form the outside of the flower while it is in bud and protect the inner parts of the bloom as they develop. These sepals are usually about equal in size; the uppermost sepal is known as the dorsal sepal and the two lower ones the lateral sepals. Next we have the three petals; the two upper petals are often similar in appearance to the sepals whereas the third, lower petal is adapted in sometimes quite a dramatic way to form the lip or labellum. This structure is basically acting as a beacon to

the insect pollinators of the flower, attracting them with its usually yellow center or yellow honey guides to steer the insect towards the nectar that will reward them for pollinating the flower. The lip is also formed in such a way as to provide a landing platform for the insects. There are many orchids that have evolved over thousands of years to a highly specialized flower structure that is geared to one specific pollinator. Some even have a particularly cunning way of trapping an insect inside until it has done its job and then can be released to freedom once again. The various slipper orchids, *Paphiopedilum*,

Phragmipedium and *Cypripedium*, are common examples of how flowers have formed to catch their prey to make sure the flower is pollinated before the insect is released. The lip has been formed into the shape of a pouch into which the insect will drop when attracted by nectar. The only route out of the slippery interior of the pouch is via a hairy path up the back which takes the insect conveniently past the pollen, through a tight exit which forces the pollen on to the insect.

Just above the lip of the flower is the column. This elongated part of the flower stem carries the stigmatic surface on its underside (where the pollen from another flower will be deposited to pollinate this flower) and the pollen on the foremost tip, covered by the anther or pollen cap. The pollen itself is held in a number of solid masses called pollinia which are bright yellow when fresh and are attached to a sticky pad that clings to

the insect's body as it visits the flower. The pollen is then deposited on the sticky stigmatic surface of the next flower that the insect visits, so pollinating that flower.

Once pollination has occurred, the orchid has no further use for its flower so the petals and sepals die off while the column starts to swell slightly as it transfers the pollen grains down towards the ova, held within the stem that attaches the flower to the flower spike. This stem is actually the ovary and is now on its way to becoming the seed capsule as the ova and pollen grains come together to form the tiny seeds. This will swell and increase in length over the following weeks and months until it becomes ripe. The time that it takes to ripen will vary between the different genera, from just a few weeks to over a year.

Above: The orchid pollen is situated right in the center of the flower, on the column, where it is easily accessible to the pollinating insect.

Below: The highly patterned lip of this flower, colored in bright reds and yellows, is the perfect guide for insects towards the pollen.

PROPAGATION

47

Left: This seed capsule on a *Cattleya* species is nearing maturity and will soon start to turn yellow and split, releasing the dust-like seeds into the air.

Right: In this *Encyclia* species the old flower parts can still be clearly seen attached to the seed capsule, several months after pollination.

Orchid Seed

Orchid seed is quite unique; it is incredibly fine, resembling golden yellow sawdust in most cases. Epiphytic species make up the vast majority of the world's orchids and with a plant existing high up in the branches of a tree, a large or heavy seed would not be suitable. Therefore, the orchid has evolved a minuscule seed in which the embryo is enclosed only by a husk that is one cell thick. This enables the seed of some orchids to be distributed by air movement between the trees, so hopefully remaining within the higher branches rather than dropping down to the forest floor. This is done gradually as the seed capsule slowly splits and opens over a period of a few weeks. As it is rather hit and miss as to whether the seed will land in just the right place, the mother plant will produce many thousands, up to one million in fact, of these seeds to ensure even just a few succeed. In their natural habitat, orchids have a special association with particular species of fungi and, within the germinating process, the orchid seed cannot develop without the presence of the fungal strands that provide the developing embryo with vital nutrients that it needs to grow.

Pollination in Cultivation

This is how it all happens in the wild, but how about when growers wish to raise seeds in the confines of their greenhouses? The flowers are pollinated by hand, using a sharpened matchstick or cocktail stick to lift and deposit the pollinia from one parent flower to another. The respective plants are then labeled with the date and details of the parents used to make the cross. This information is usually also recorded in a stud book. Once the seed has ripened it must be sown immediately and the standard way uses modern techniques in sterile laboratory conditions. The seed must first be sterilized itself and then sown on to a specially formulated agar gel which contains all the nutrients necessary for germination; this gel bypasses what the fungus does in nature. This is all contained within a sterile glass jar that is kept in a temperature- and light-controlled environment.

As the seed germinates, the embryo turns into a ball of green cells called a protocorm. This can photosynthesize (produce the energy it needs from sunlight) and continues to increase in size until it reaches the point when it is large enough to start producing its first leaf and roots. The tiny orchid plant is then starting to take shape, producing more leaves and roots as it grows. When these leaves start to grow, the tiny seedlings are thinned out and transferred to another sterile jar containing a slightly different gel. Growers have many different recipes for this gel but the most common additives are banana and charcoal, which suit different orchids that prefer a little added potassium or carbon. Coconut, potato, tomato, and pineapple have also been used to boost the orchids' growth over these important months. The young plants will then stay in this second jar until they reach the top and are strong enough to survive the outside world. A plant that has healthy green leaves, perhaps even its first tiny pseudobulb, and a strong root system has a much better chance of survival than a small, weak plant, so it is important to leave the plants in the jars for as long as possible.

The plants are removed from the glass jars with care, as they are quite fragile and can snap easily. They are briefly rinsed in a fungicidal solution to prevent them becoming victims to the fungal spores ever present in the air around them. Then they are potted into a community seed tray, preferably one with cells for individual plants so that if one does die then any disease will not be easily passed on to its neighbor. As the plants have a very fine root system, a fine, moist soil mixture is best for them at this first stage. A mixture of fine grade bark, perlite for drainage, and peat or sphagnum moss for moisture, is an ideal seedling soil. The plants are then kept in a warm, humid environment and regularly misted to prevent them from drying out too much.

At this stage the orchids will be around one year old and they can take several more years of annual repotting until they reach flowering size, usually four to five years in total from seed to flowering plant. With sympodial orchids, the pseudobulbs increase in size each year until they are large enough to make their first flower spike. From this point onwards, they will carry on growing and flowering year after year, indefinitely. Monopodial orchids will continue to increase the size of their leaves until they reach their optimum size.

HYBRIDIZATION

The Early Days

As we have already seen, mankind's association with orchids stretches back many thousands of years into pre-history. We know the interest in these plants has always been there alongside all other forms of horticulture.

However, the selective breeding of plants and an understanding of hybridizing clearly began in the eighteenth century. In the early Victorian times, at the height of orchid mania, various experts were wondering what would happen if hybridization was attempted between different species that they had in their collections.

The firm of Veitch & Sons in Exeter, England, one of the largest nurseries in the world at that time, employed collectors on every continent to send back new plants, seeds, and bulbs to their nursery. Here they had a large collection of orchids and the head grower was a local man, John Dominy. In the late 1840s John Dominy was working with a surgeon called John Harris, who was also a botanist and studied the anatomy of orchid flowers in great depth. With his help, Dominy set about pollinating various orchid flowers and by experimenting with closely related species and cross-pollinating them, some of their results were successful and some failed. They soon learned that if the cross succeeded and produced a large seed capsule, it would contain many thousands of seeds. The orchid seed, being extremely fine, was difficult to grow without a complete understanding of its requirements. Unfortunately, John Dominy did not keep exact records of his early attempts but we may assume that he crossed many different orchids in the collection to decide which would produce seed.

The most attractive were the large, colorful cattleyas from South America and it was these that they first tried to cross-pollinate. The resulting seedlings proved very slow to grow and were to take many years before they finally flowered. While waiting for them to grow, they continued pollinating other flowers, among which were some of the evergreen calanthes. These proved to be very fertile and gave large quantities of seed which, when sown, was quicker to reach maturity and flower. These

Right: This *Cymbidium* hybrid is a result of many years of complex hybridization.

seedlings overtook those of the cattleyas that had been raised earlier and so it was that in 1856 the first calanthes flowered. They caused a great sensation in the orchid world when the first hybrid, a cross between *Calanthe furcata* and *C. masuca* was named in honor of John Dominy, *Calanthe* 'Dominii' (see page 110).

Dominy's work in hybridization was to continue throughout his life. During that time he was to make many orchid hybrids, experimenting with all the major genera then in cultivation, but he was always faced with the problem of large quantities of seed and poor germination. His successor at Veitch & Sons was a man called John Seden who was to carry on the successful line of breeding with even more genera.

The early Victorians believed that it would not be possible to raise second or third generation hybrids and they were certain that once two species had been crossed the resulting plants would be sterile. They called this the "muling of orchids," but to their surprise, they discovered that it was possible to continue breeding from their hybrids into a second and third generation. Not only was this possible but they were able to make extremely wide crosses, interbreeding different genera successfully, a practice not possible with many other types of plant.

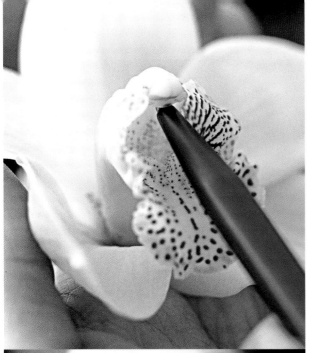

Top left: Using a blunt instrument, such as a cocktail stick or pen nib, remove the pollen from the first orchid flower.

Left: The pollen from this *Cymbidium* flower will stick to the blunt instrument, while covered by the pollen cap.

Below left: Knock off the pollen cap to reveal the bright orange pollen sacks.

Right: Insert the pollen into the sticky stigmatic surface behind the pollen on the next flower being used to make the cross. Then repeat the process in reverse.

Right:
Bulbophyllum
'Jersey'.

Left:
Phragmipedium
'Longueville'.

Far Right:
Dendrobium
'Pink Beauty'.

The Naming of Hybrids

By the turn of the century, fifty years after Dominy started hybridizing, many people were successfully raising seedlings both in England and France and success too had come to the east coast of America. Up until now, all hybrids had been passed to botanists such as the Institute of the Royal Botanic Gardens at Kew, England, for naming and classifying. Early hybrids from that time were usually given a Latin name, the same as a species, but all this was to change and the growers were allowed to give their hybrids their own choice of name.

Sanders of St. Albans, England, was a very large orchid establishment at that time and Frederick Sander invited all producers of new hybrids to record their names with him. He would then list the names in a publication, on a first come, first served basis and once a cross had been given a chosen name, that name would last for all time. Any subsequent crosses of the same parents would automatically bear the name that had been registered with Sander. This method continued until January 1, 1961, when the task of registration was taken over by the Royal Horticultural Society in London.

By the end of the twentieth century, over 100,000 hybrids had been registered, with new ones being created at the rate of 3,000 a year. This number increases year by year, as all over the world orchid hybridizers are producing new plants. Until recently, the new hybrids were published every five years but now with so many hybrids being registered this happens more often, as well as the complete register being available on CD-ROM. This means that a hybridizer can trace the lineage of his plants all the way back to the original species, discovering who registered the crosses and the dates on which they were made. This has proved to be an invaluable scientific work, unparalleled in any other form of horticulture. Although far from complete, as down through the years many growers have failed to register unsuccessful crosses, important parents have always been recorded and these are the lines of breeding that count when the hybridizer sets to work. With some hybrids it is possible to trace their parentage right back to the early work done in the nineteenth century and to still find that the plants are fertile. With selective breeding and understanding of the genetic make-up of hybrids, it is possible to produce intergeneric hybrids containing six, seven, or even eight genera all rolled into one.

Left:
Vuylstekeara
'Cambria Plush'.

Right: *Odontioda*
'Garnet'.

Far right:
Cymbidium
'Ming Pagoda'.

Hybridizing Today

Today the hybridizer needs a good knowledge of genetics, a subject of which the Victorians knew little. Their idea of hybridizing was simply to cross two different flowers on a hit or miss basis to see if any seed was produced. Now we understand that the blueprints of life are carried in the chromosomes of both parents. Most orchid species have pairs of chromosomes and are called diploid—they will freely breed with one another. Occasionally, a plant with double the usual number of chromosomes, a tetraploid, will appear. If a tetraploid is crossed with a diploid the number of chromosomes is doubled, improving the shape, size, and quality of flowers, also usually affecting the vigor of the plant. A plant with an uneven number of chromosomes will not cross with another, but it is possible today to convert plants, even of a hybrid 100 years old, which have never before been able to breed. By changing their chromosome numbers they can be turned into breeding plants and thus the lineage of hybridizing will continue for many more generations. It seems certain that, with the help of science, the future of orchid breeding will change. Plants and colors hitherto unimagined will be available. The purpose of hybridization is to produce new colors, new shapes, and more vigorous plants, better than any that have gone before. Of the 25,000 different species of orchids, very few of them have been bred from and it is those few of the most popular genera that are responsible for the many hybrids available today.

There are two main types of hybridizer: the commercial nurseryman who breeds purely for a definite market, producing new hybrids for the potted plant and cut flower trade, for important days such as Christmas, Easter, and Mother's Day, when the demand is at its peak, and the speculative breeder who is always looking for something new and unusual. These are mainly the leading amateurs who take a great deal of time and trouble investing in experimental hybridizing. These breeders receive many awards and prizes and their results are much admired by other growers and collectors of the unusual. The results of all this hard work can be seen when visiting an orchid show, a dazzling display of exceptional plants all due to the hybridizer's art.

Pests and Diseases

PESTS

Growing orchids in a greenhouse or on the window sill means that they are naturally isolated from the common pests that abound in our gardens, so a greenhouse full of plants remains immune from most infestations without any serious problems. However, once a pest has entered the greenhouse, the environment that has been paradise for the orchids becomes paradise for the pests. With no natural predators to control them, pests and diseases can quickly become rampant and infect the whole of the collection. Keeping a careful eye out for pests and preventing an attack is better than trying to cure a heavy infestation. If you know in advance what type of pest is likely to attack a specific orchid then routine inspection of your plants will spot an early arrival. The trouble can then be under immediate control before it has time to spread.

Certain plants will always play host to specific insects and it is possible, in a mixed greenhouse, to have orchids alongside many other plants. The pest will often be apparent on one plant before it spreads to others. For example, if fuchsias are grown with orchids then white fly will almost certainly be present; it will not attack the orchids but will only be attracted to the fuchsias.

If you choose chemical insecticides to control pests, it is important that you follow the manufacturer's instructions to the letter. Using insecticides stronger than recommended, mixing different types together, or using old preparations that have been on the shelf for too long is not advisable. It is difficult and inappropriate to use insecticides in the home, where children or pets could be affected.

Over the years, many strong insecticides that were considered safe have been withdrawn and are no longer available. It is, therefore, important to use a non-chemical means of control whenever possible and we will recommend the safest method for each individual pest.

There are two ways of introducing pests into your orchid collection. One is by bringing in infected plants. It is very important, therefore, to check over every orchid and all other plants new to the greenhouse. Each one

Below: Mice can be a problem if they get into your greenhouse, stealing pollen from the flowers and even chewing the pseudobulbs.

should be examined carefully and if in doubt, quarantine it for a while before introducing it to the rest of the collection. Buying from a reputable nursery does not always mean that the plants will be free from pests. Even in the best establishments there can lurk the odd red spider mite or mealy bug waiting to spread through a collection.

The other enemy is the garden surrounding the greenhouse, which will be full of natural pests. For example, aphids will breed happily throughout the summer on your roses and red spider mite may infest your apple trees in late summer. Most of these pests are tolerated in the garden, with the knowledge that the coming winter will drive them into hibernation and reduce their numbers drastically. However, this will not happen in a greenhouse.

Ventilators or doors left open on a warm summer's night will allow slugs and snails to crawl into the greenhouse and make themselves at home in the moist, humid conditions. For all these reasons the grower must be forever vigilant and remember that prevention is better than cure.

Red Spider Mite

This name is a slight misnomer as it is not red nor a spider, but an extremely small mite just visible to the naked eye. It attacks certain types of orchids more than others. The most plagued plant is the cymbidium; red spider mite attacks the undersides of the leaves where in nature it would be safe from predators and rain. These microscopic pests, as individuals, do little harm but if the greenhouse is kept too dry then the pest can quickly multiply to plague proportions. When a plant becomes infested, the undersides of the leaves turn a silvery grey and then the mites will begin to attack flower buds and blooms alike. The sheer number of mites greatly reduces the strength of the plant, by damaging the leaves to such an extent that it prevents the plant from breathing properly. The problem is worst in the spring and summer, as the mites overwinter as eggs. Red spider mite will attack other orchids such as dendrobiums, some of the *Odontoglossum* family, and soft-leaved orchids such as lycastes, thunias, and calanthes. It seldom does harm to harder-leaved orchids such as cattleyas and laelias.

The best form of control is humidity and when spraying the foliage on hot summer days, direct the mist from the sprayer or hose on the underneath of the leaves as well as the top surface. Water is the red spider mite's greatest enemy. It is not unusual in a large

collection of cymbidiums to find the pest present, particularly on those plants that are at the back of the bench or seldom examined properly. To treat a heavily infested cymbidium, use a bowl of water with some horticultural soap or dish detergent and a sponge. Wipe every leaf individually and repeat several times to get the pest under control.

Many pests can be controlled with biological methods. This involves introducing the pest's natural predator to control it. Red spider mite can be controlled using a predatory mite. These mites can be purchased from companies that produce them for the horticultural industry. They are released into the greenhouse to attack and devour the red spider mites. The problem with this form of biological control is that once the predator has reduced the pest by significant numbers, it dies out itself so

Above left: To prevent and eradicate red spider mite, sponge the leaves regularly on both sides with mild soapy water.

Above right: The microscopic red spider mite can be found mostly on the undersides of leaves when the growing conditions are too warm and dry.

constant reintroduction is necessary. This type of control is only effective on large collections of plants. It seems to work best on crops such as tomatoes and cucumbers that are difficult to spray with insecticide. In the case of an amateur collection of cymbidiums, regular spraying and washing of the foliage with water seems to be the best method.

If insecticides can be used safely, the best are the systemic types that are taken up by the plant and poison the mites when they chew through the foliage. These can be sprayed on to the foliage several times a year, before the pest is detected. They inoculate the plant against the pest and have a lasting effect. They are an excellent means of control where it is safe to use them.

False Spider Mite

There is an even smaller pest known as false spider mite or phalaenopsis mite. This, as its name suggests, attacks phalaenopsis more than any other orchid. The results can be seen on both the tops and undersides of the leaves, where the cells collapse leaving deep pits in a patchwork across the foliage. This pest is very hard to see with the naked eye and usually needs the aid of a strong magnifying glass. It thrives, like other mites, in dry conditions and can affect plants grown on a window sill or in a dry conservatory where it can quickly spread from one orchid to another. At the first sign of infection immediate treatment is necessary, using the methods recommended for red spider mite. If the plant can spare the foliage, a good idea is to trim the affected leaves off altogether.

Mealy Bug and Scale Insects

These pests are related to one another and belong to a large group of insects that includes many species that attack orchids. We do not need to know the differences between them; to the orchid grower they are just pests to be controlled. The scale insects can take on many forms; some are hard, black, horny insects that attach themselves to the undersides of the leaves, while others are quite soft and easily squashed.

Most of these insects have a larval stage, at which they are very small and seldom seen by the orchid grower. We are first aware of their presence when we examine the orchids and find, hidden on the undersides of the leaves, large patches of these hard, scaly insects, some of them covering themselves with a white, mealy powder. It is a pest that will attack most orchids but cattleyas and their related hybrids in particular. The insects are usually hiding on the undersides of the leaves or beneath the bracts which sheathe the bulbs and new growths. If they remain undetected they can reduce the strength of a plant and quickly kill it.

Different types of scale insects can be specific to different orchid genera. One type is only found on cattleyas but is unlikely to attack cymbidiums and vice versa. Mealy bugs, of which there are a number of different species, will also attack a wide range of orchids. They are far more mobile than scale insects and have a white, fluffy appearance. They will spread quickly all over a plant and are very fond of phalaenopsis, not only attacking the underside of the leaves but gathering around the center of the flowers and hiding between the petals. It is always a shock to see newly opened blooms already contaminated with mealy bug which has been hiding behind the unopened bud waiting to crawl into the flower. Once they have infested flowers, it is very difficult to eliminate them. If the blooms are badly infested it is best to remove the flowers rather than spend time trying to clean them. Examining the underside of phalaenopsis leaves on a regular basis will act as prevention; remember, also, to keep an eye on the growing flower spikes before the blooms open for the tell-tale signs of white fluffy specks.

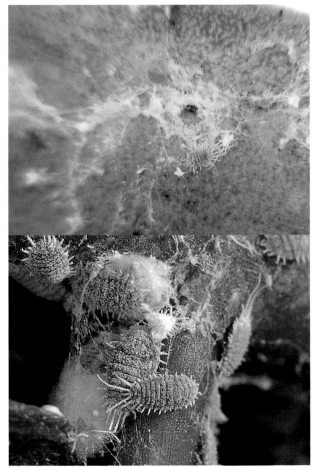

Top right: Mealy bug will start off as a fine web of a white, fluffy substance, usually on the undersides of leaves or in hidden nooks and crannies.

Bottom right: Individual mealy bugs are quite mobile and easily visible when out in the open. They will congregate in clusters and feed on the sap of the orchid.

It is possible to obtain a biological control for these pests, a type of ladybug which will predate only mealy bugs. However, as always with biological control there is the danger that the predator will starve to death before it has finally annihilated the pest. Horticultural soap is very effective, as both mealy bugs and scale insects have a greasy protective covering. Once this defense mechanism has broken down, the insect is very vulnerable and quickly dies. Washing the plant with horticultural soap or rubbing alcohol can be an effective means of control. Where a collection of cattleyas is badly affected by scale insects, it can take many months to finally get rid of them, but you must persist with the treatment before the insects get the upper hand.

Most scale insects and mealy bugs are tropical pests and are not found in the wild in the cooler parts of the world. They are, therefore, usually introduced into a collection on infected plants.

Slugs and Snails

Both these pests can be a real nuisance in the greenhouse, slipping in from outside unexpectedly. Most orchids produce a tough leaf that does not make interesting eating but they are very interested in the flower spikes and buds. Somehow they have the habit of being able to track down a tasty flower spike from a great distance. If there is only one flower spike in the greenhouse, you can be sure that a slug or snail will find it; if there are a dozen or more buds and flowers, the pest will go from one bloom to another taking a bite here and there, rather than being content with just one flower, thus ruining the whole appearance in one night.

The only orchid foliage they like is the soft succulent leaves of phalaenopsis and it is so distressing to go into the greenhouse in the morning to find large, circular holes eaten through the leaves of your prize plant. They also like orchid roots and eat the young, tender tips.

The best method of controlling slugs and snails is to keep the greenhouse clean and tidy to prevent them from finding a suitable home in the first place. Flower spikes can be protected by wrapping a band of cotton wool around the base of the spike and the supporting bamboo cane. These mollusks find it impossible to get a hold on this fluffy surface and so cannot cross it. Seeking them out after dark, with a torch, will usually uncover the culprit out for his nightly feast.

There is also a small, black, round snail known as a garlic or moss snail. It frequently breeds in the soil and can be a great nuisance in the seedling house, where it will damage the roots of young plants. Lay slices of apple, potato, or even orange peel on the surface of the soil and look under them each morning; you will find the pests hiding underneath where they have enjoyed a meal of the sweet fruit. You can then discard the culprits.

Slugs and snails can also be baited or sprayed but this should not be necessary if you look out for them regularly. Cymbidiums that have been placed in the garden for the summer will be returned to the greenhouse with the pests hiding in the crock holes at the bottom of the pot or in the surface of the soil. Stand the plants in water up to the rim of the pot for half an hour before returning them to the greenhouse. This will drown any slugs, snails, or other pests that have made their home in the pot.

Above: Slugs and snails can wreak havoc, especially on the softer parts of the orchid such as new flower stems, buds, and new leaves. This large garden snail may find its way into your greenhouse in cold weather, smaller types may live there permanently.

Aphids

There are many different species of this pest, collectively known as greenfly. They seldom harm the plants themselves as they find the leaves too tough, except for some soft-leaved orchids such as lycastes and calanthes. When they do attack the foliage of these plants, it is usually on the underside of the leaf. These orchids have very tender leaves and are therefore susceptible to insecticide spray. In a collection consisting of just a few plants, the easiest method of control is to lay the orchid on its side, exposing the undersides of the leaves, and wipe off the pest with a wet cloth, repeating whenever necessary, at the first sign.

Greenfly most often attack orchid flowers and buds. These pests have the ability to breed at an alarming rate and within days, a few insects will have multiplied to many dozens or even hundreds more. The buds are the most susceptible part of the flower's anatomy and any insecticide used here will damage the buds even more than the pest, causing them to turn yellow and drop off. At the first sign of aphids nestling among the young buds, wash them off immediately with water. However,

Above: Greenfly will quickly multiply into large numbers if left undisturbed. They can cause great damage to young leaves or flower buds.

Right: The larvae of the vine weevil is most destructive to the orchid roots but the adults will also eat young leaves after dark.

damage will have already been done and when the flowers finally open, the petals will show blemishes which have grown with the expanding petals. If the sprays of flowers are heavily infested with aphids hiding among the folds of the petals and in the throats of the blooms, it is best to remove the whole spike to prevent the greenfly spreading to other flowers in the greenhouse. As with other sap-sucking insects, it is possible to use systemic insecticide which will give long-term inoculation to the plant. This is not safe to use on soft-leaved lycastes and vigilance is the best method of control.

Vine Weevils

One of the most common garden pests is the vine weevil. It thrives in pots of plants such as cyclamen where it devastates everything it comes in contact with, both the larvae and the adult weevil attacking the plant. Fortunately there have been few reports of them causing damage to orchids but if they do become established in the pot, the larvae will quickly eat the orchid roots. As with all pests of this nature the best method of control is quick action. Repot the plant completely, removing all old soil and washing it under a running tap, then allowing it to dry. Then thoroughly examine the plant making sure there are no larvae burrowing in the roots or tucked into the root ball. All old soil should be disposed of carefully. Weevils can be sprayed with insecticide but they are resistant to the most commonly available cures.

Ants

Ants themselves do little or no harm to orchids and when they are seen running up and down a flower spike it is usually because they are visiting the blooms for their nectar. They can be seen gathering around the back of the flower and at the joint with the stem. Here, in many species of orchids, is where much nectar is secreted. They can be more of a nuisance than a pest and where greenfly infestations occur, the ants can be found encouraging this pest as they feed off the sweet honeydew that many aphids produce. Ants can travel great distances from their nest in the garden to a warm greenhouse where they will set up home in the orchid pots. They can be easily controlled by setting traps for them across their trails without using insecticides or poisons. When a nest is established in your favorite cymbidium pot, immerse the whole thing in water for half an hour.

Moss Flies

Moss flies are small insects which breed rapidly in certain types of orchid soil, particularly where peat or moss has been used. They have a fast breeding rate and stay close to the pot in which they were born. They do little or no harm to mature orchids, but where large infestations occur in seedling or community pots they can damage the young roots. The adult moss fly is a poor flyer and therefore does not travel far, usually returning to the pot in which it was bred to produce another generation. These and other small flying insects, such as gnats and thrips, together with ants, can all be controlled by growing insectivorous plants among your orchids. The butterworts and sundews, with their sticky leaves, give an added interest to the grower and are an effective means of control.

Above: Keep bumble bees away from your orchid flowers as they will easily knock off the pollen, so shortening the bloom's life.

Woodlice

Woodlice are common garden pests; turn over any stone or piece of wood and you will find a large family. They infest our compost heaps where they do a lot of good, breaking down the plant material. In the greenhouse, however, they can be a nuisance, attacking plant roots undetected as they quietly enter the crock holes in the bottom of the pot. They seem immune to most poisons and baits as their digestive system is very poor. The best method of controlling them is to maintain a high standard of cleanliness both inside and outside the greenhouse. Any unwanted plant material and any dirty pots should not be stored on the floor but removed at once. As with other pests, if you suspect a large colony is breeding in the soil, either repot the plant or soak it in water for half an hour and the problem will be solved.

Bumble Bees

These large, beautiful, noisy insects can be a considerable nuisance to orchid growers, especially in the early spring when the bees come out of hibernation to find there are no flowers waiting for them. The hungry insects soon smell the cymbidiums and, once in the greenhouse, happily travel from flower to flower. Each time they visit they pollinate the blooms and within a few days many cymbidium flowers start collapsing. To prevent these insects from coming inside at this time of the year, the vents should be gauzed and the door kept shut. Any other openings should be covered in a similar way.

Mice

Mice find their way into a greenhouse through any small hole or crack near to the ground. Once in the warm comfortable conditions they quickly make themselves at home. They will not attack the orchids directly but are always interested in soft, tender flower buds and the pollen on fresh flowers, which they find very nutritious. It is possible, in a single night, for a small family of mice to remove all the pollen on your orchids, doing an immense amount of damage and shortening the life of the flowers. They always strike when least expected.

PREVENTION OF DISEASES

All orchids, whether in cultivation in a greenhouse, in a tropical garden, or even in their wild state, can be subject to various fungal or bacterial infections. Gardeners in hot countries, where it is safe to grow orchids out of doors, dose their plants regularly with strong concentrations of bactericide or fungicide preparations. In tropical conditions, such infections will spread rapidly through a collection of plants, moving from one to another. Prevention is, once again, the key word.

In cooler climates, where most of us grow our orchids, in greenhouses or on the window sill, we can still be annoyed by various diseases. They are particularly troublesome in seedling houses, where once a rot starts to infect a seed tray it will quickly spread to the rest of the plants. If your pot-grown orchids begin to rot for no apparent reason they can quickly decay until they are beyond saving. Where do these infections and fungi come from? Some are air or water borne and can be introduced to your plants by these methods. Where a greenhouse is kept scrupulously clean and no rubbish is allowed to remain on the floor or benches, the spores from other decaying material are less likely to spread to the orchids. Even a compost heap close to the greenhouse can be a source of infection. Hygiene is better than cure, and healthy, fit plants will fight off an infection naturally. A greenhouse where rubbish is allowed to accumulate, combined with a winter of low temperatures and high humidity, can only become a breeding ground for problems.

In the past, it has been a bad habit of orchid growers to have water tanks under the benches. During watering, the surplus water runs back through the slats in the benches into the tanks underneath. This seems to be a good water-saving idea in dry summers. However, re-cycling the water through the plants over and over again can bring a real risk of water-borne diseases building up in the warm greenhouse. Each time the plant is watered, you are re-introducing the infection and it will soon reach a stage when it is impossible to combat the bacteria. A rain water tank outside the greenhouse will have the same effect, particularly if nearby trees shed their leaves into the tank. The use of soft water is recommended, rather than hard rain water. Even soft rain water that has been stored for long periods and recycled constantly, as described, will be more harmful than tap water.

The problem usually starts in the autumn or winter when the orchids' growth rate has slowed down. Low temperatures, combined with too much moisture for plants that should be resting or growing very slowly, will quickly set up an infection at the base of the growth. Basal rot, once begun, is difficult to stop and will spread right through the plant. Young seedlings, not long out of the laboratory, are easily infected. The whole tray can damp off within a few days. Soft-leaved orchids such as *Phalaenopsis* are very prone to rots which run rapidly through their foliage and these bulbless orchids are quickly destroyed. Provided resting orchids are kept dry in the winter, given plenty of air movement and good light, the problem will not arise. *Miltoniopsis* and *Phalaenopsis* that grow all the year round must be kept warm to prevent infections.

Flowers and buds can also be infected at this time of the year. Large white *Phalaenopsis* very quickly show damp spots if left for two or three nights in a low temperature.

Cymbidium and *Phalaenopsis* buds are very susceptible to low light levels. During the darkest of the winter months, several days or weeks with no sunshine at all result in the buds turning yellow and dropping off. The check of these conditions is just too much for them. Keeping the plants warmer to counteract the poor light will have the reverse effect, for while they can stand the heat in the summer when the light is good, they do not like poor light combined with heat. Some growers try to supplement the light levels with artificial light but this is only successful with certain types of orchid, such as *Phalaenopsis* and *Cattleya*. Artificial light has little effect on cymbidiums.

Once a plant shows signs of rot at the base of the new growth or bulb it is essential that the affected parts are quickly removed. Clean back to healthy material and treat with any of the fungicides or bactericides that are available. Flowers of sulfur can be used to help prevent the disease from spreading or occurring again. Be careful not to overdose with fungicide as this can act as a growth retardant. Cut back affected *Phalaenopsis* leaves with a sharp knife, then dry the edge and paint with fungicide. All cutting tools must be regularly cleaned between each cut, either with a flame or disinfectant.

Flowers that have become spotted are best removed to allow the plant to go back into growth and flower again later when the plant is healthier. Maintaining the right temperature, with the use of a small fan to assist in air movement on cold winter nights and long cloudy days, is the best method of keeping these problems at bay. Orchids growing on a window sill are better off in the dryer conditions found indoors and, as a result, have less chance of contamination.

VIRUSES

Viruses are one of the most common causes of illness throughout both the animal and plant kingdoms. These microscopic organisms affect the very life system of a plant. They can invade the cells and do untold harm, resulting in deformed foliage, badly marked leaves, and poor quality flowers showing severe color breaking and uneven patterning. The debilitating effect on the plant can result in its final demise. There are many sorts of virus that infect our orchids and some varieties are more prone to attack than others. *Phalaenopsis*, for example, become affected for no apparent reason perhaps due to their soft leaves while other orchids, such as cymbidiums, which are very prone to viruses, will linger on for years with no effect. Other plants still, such as coelogynes, growing alongside may not be affected at all.

Viruses that affect cymbidiums first become noticed in the new growth, showing lighter patches of green and forming a pattern as the growth develops. With age these patches die, leaving dead cells to be infected with bacteria or fungus, giving a mottled effect with black spots over the leaves. Such viruses are totally incurable; there is no known treatment or cure. The only method is instant disposal of the plant and its pot to prevent the virus spreading to the other orchids. Viruses are slow to spread from plant to plant but the usual method is by way of sap-sucking insect pests, such as red spider mite, which will quickly travel through a collection of cymbidiums transmitting the virus from one plant to the next. Old collections of cymbidiums are often found to be infected with both red spider mite and viruses and such collections can only be disposed of. If this is not done, any new plants introduced will quickly become infected too. The other way of spreading the disease is by pruning shears or scissors when trimming foliage or roots and cutting flowers. When carrying out such work, even on the cleanest of plants, it is essential to keep the cutting tools regularly sterilized.

The amateur who has bought clean healthy stock from a reliable source is unlikely to encounter a virus and should not become alarmed by the slightest mark on old foliage. Orchids that keep their leaves for many years will naturally start to deteriorate, showing black tipping and signs of die back. When these leaves fall from the plant they should be immediately removed to the outside of the greenhouse.

Where do viruses come from and how do they invade our orchid plants? Experts tell us that they are not transmittable by seed and that seed produced by an affected plant that is dried before sowing will not carry forward the infection. It is possible that most orchids have viruses lying dormant in their leaves and when the plant gets stressed through neglect or severe conditions, then the viruses appear. Years ago it was thought that if infected cymbidiums were kept very warm they would be cured. This is not true; the plants just grow faster and softer so that the virus is less visible.

Top left: To prevent slugs and snails reaching the flower buds, tie some cotton wool around the base of the flower spike as this is difficult for the pests to cross.

Bottom left: This *Phalaenopsis* is showing symptoms of having been kept too wet. The leaves are starting to turn yellow and brown and eventually they will all drop off. It is often difficult to revive a plant once this has happened.

Popular Plants

CATTLEYA ALLIANCE

The *Cattleya* Alliance is a huge group of orchids. Botanically, they belong to the sub-tribe *Laelineae* which includes the genera *Cattleya*, *Laelia*, *Sophronitis*, *Brassavola*, *Encyclia*, *Epidendrum*, and many, many others. Where hybrids are concerned within this group they are always referred to collectively as cattleyas.

Their native homes are throughout tropical South America and as far north as Mexico. Some species come from the West Indies. The biggest, most flamboyant plants come from the coastal mountains of Brazil. These orchids have had a great influence on hybridization, producing a tremendous amount of new flowers. The largest are almost the size of a dinner plate, in many colors, which will last many weeks in perfection. The smallest are tiny, brightly colored jewels.

Hybrids were first made 150 years ago and cattleyas were the first tropical orchids to be hybridized and successfully brought into flower. They have always dominated the orchid scene, being the ultimate in large, showy flowers. The first plant, a specimen of *Cattleya labiata*, arrived into cultivation in 1818 as packing material and flowered in the collection of Mr. Cattley in South London, England. He recognized the plant as being different from anything he had seen before and so carefully nurtured it until it flowered. It caused a huge sensation and the taxonomists of the day named it after Mr. Cattley. His name has been remembered ever since and while other orchids have been named after their discoverers, few have achieved such fame as the *Cattleya*. With the flowering of this first plant, interest in orchids was to take a giant turn. Everyone wanted to know more about these exotic flowers. Collectors were dispatched to

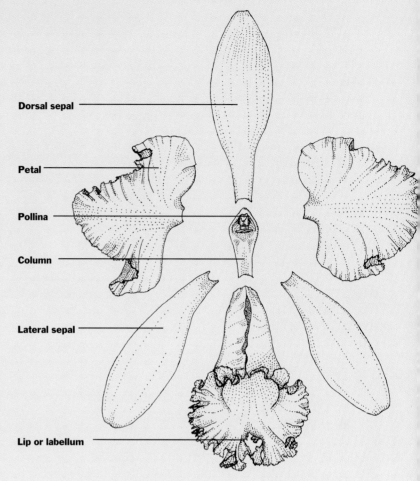

Above: The *Cattleya* flower dissected to show all the flower parts.

every part of South America, where they plundered the jungles for new and different varieties, shipping them back by the boatload to the British Isles, to meet the insatiable demand for this, the largest and showiest of all orchids. There are many stories of how these orchids were collected, found growing in great clumps in forks of gigantic trees or covering whole hillsides growing on rocky outcrops, and how the rarest, white varieties were found growing in great profusion on church roofs.

Until the 1930s, fashionable ladies wore orchids as corsages, in their hair or on their hats. Cattleyas were greatly sought after; the larger and showier the bloom, the more popular they were. When the fashion declined, interest waned and now cattleyas are grown more for their beauty as a plant than for the cut flower trade.

Fully mature plants that are exhibited bearing several flower heads never fail to attract the eye to their bright colors. Their popularity today seems greatest in North America, where amateurs grow them in large greenhouses, as they are not easily accommodated in a small space. Because the flowers are not so long-lived as those of other orchids and are strictly seasonal, they have not been successful in the potted plant market and still remain in the domain of the collectors of the rare and unusual.

They produce a large, stout pseudobulb, from the top of which come one, two, or sometimes three thick, leathery leaves. These plants, growing as large groups of pseudobulbs, flower from the newest growth. Blooms are produced from inside a sheath, which forms at the top of the pseudobulb between the foliage, usually in heads of two, three, or sometimes up to five flowers. This growth habit is much the same for the closely related genus *Laelia. Sophronitis* is a genus of small, compact plants with bright red flowers; when crossed with laelias and cattleyas it introduces color and a shorter stature.

Cultivation and Care

Many of the species are seldom grown today, as some of them prove difficult and specialized in their watering and cultural requirements. Colorful hybrids are easier to grow and are greatly sought after. Due to the complex interbreeding that has taken place, it is not easy to determine their particular flowering season. A mixed collection of plants can be growing and flowering at almost any time of the year. Their cycle means that the new growth will start from the base of the leading pseudobulb. When the new growth is half completed there is a massive production of new roots from the base. Plenty of water and fertilizer must be given at this time to encourage the largest pseudobulb and leaves possible. The aim is to make the growth at least the size of the previous season's, if not bigger.

Once the new growth has completed, the flowering sheath will bloom. The end result is the best, healthiest flowers that the plant is capable of producing. Most cattleyas flower while they are resting, so give them less water during this period.

It is best to repot these plants as soon as the flowers have finished and before the next season's growth has started, especially if the leading pseudobulb has reached the edge of the pot or has crept over it.

In the winter months, these orchids can take full light; their hard leaves enjoy the bright, cool sunshine. As the spring progresses, the reverse can happen and the leaves can easily overheat causing severe scorching. It is important, from this time until the autumn, to provide adequate shade. Cattleyas grown in too much light will be short with harder, more yellow foliage. They may give better blooms but at the expense of the appearance of the plant. It is always the object of a good grower to obtain an even balance between flowering and growing.

Due to their breeding, some of this group of orchids are capable of standing lower temperatures than others. Those that have Mexican *Laelia* or *Cattleya* species in their background are liable to be more tolerant of low temperatures. The hardiest will withstand a temperature of 55° F (12° C). In a mixed collection it is safer to keep them all at a minimum of 60° F (15° C). These should be the lowest temperatures on the coldest of winter nights and one would expect a much higher nighttime temperature during the summer when the plants are active. The daytime temperatures should be correspondingly higher. If the

Above: *Cattleya bowringiana.*

Below: *Cattleya skinneri.*

sun comes out then the temperature in the greenhouse will automatically rise. Even on the shortest of winter days a little sunshine will quickly lift the temperature by a considerable amount, although not enough to require ventilation. On hot summer days the plants will benefit from extra ventilation and the fresh air, combined with shading from direct sun, will provide ideal growing conditions. The plants should never be allowed to become completely dry. Although there are many different kinds of orchid soils, cattleyas do best in coarse, chunky bark through which their long, white rambling root systems can take firm hold.

All this adds up to the greatest group of orchids in the world and certainly the family would be poorer without the cattleyas for us all to enjoy.

Cattleya bowringiana
This species is very rewarding as it tends to produce a large head of blooms, sometimes up to 20 on a mature specimen, which gives a superb show in the winter months. The deep purple flower has an even darker lip and is shaped like a trumpet, with a contrasting white throat in the center of the tubular lip. The tall, slender pseudobulbs have a pair of leaves at the top. The attractive deep green foliage requires good light to help the plant flower well year after year. Like all cattleyas, this species from Honduras needs a minimum of 55° F (12° C) in the winter, so take care not to let them get too cool.

Cattleya skinneri
At first glance this species is fairly similar to *C. bowringiana*, but in fact it makes a shorter-growing plant and produces larger flowers in beautiful shades of lavender-purple, with dark lips. The long-lasting flowers are held on heads of up to eight. It is a popular orchid, due to its compact habit and attractive blooms. There is also a pure white variety, *C. skinneri* var. *alba*, which is also very popular but increasingly rare. This is a widespread species, first found growing in Guatemala and now well-known as the national flower of Costa Rica.

Cattleya trianae

This is one of the best known of the unifoliate cattleyas. These types have only one leaf produced from the top of each pseudobulb and because of this they often appear very similar to many of the *Laelia* species. The incredible flowers are very large, sometimes reaching 8 in. (20 cm) across. The species is quite variable but generally the color tends to be a soft, delicate pink or white, with a deeper lip that is large and frilled along the edge. The size, long-lasting quality, and beautiful fragrance of these flowers have been used extensively in the breeding of many of the modern *Cattleya* Alliance hybrids, so it is usually easier to obtain *C. trianae* hybrids than the species itself.

Cattleya harrisoniae x 'Penny Kuroda'

Some of the cattleyas, including this hybrid, have a slightly different flower with a fiddle-shaped lip. The distinctive flower shape is quite clear and the unusual earthy, reddish-pink coloring of the bloom certainly makes it stand out in a crowd. These types also have a much taller and thinner pseudobulb with a pair of leaves at the top.

Above: *Cattleya harrisoniae* x 'Penny Kuroda'.

Below left: *Cattleya* 'Louis' and 'Carla'.

Below right: *Laeliocattleya* 'Chine'.

Far right: *Cattleya trianae.*

Cattleya 'Louis' and 'Carla'

The larger-than-life blooms of the ever-popular white *Cattleya* hybrids have always been in favor, and this hybrid is no exception. In the heyday of corsage-wearing, these orchids were at their height but now they are grown more for the pleasure of the growing and flowering plants. The pure color, with only a hint of yellow in the throat, is very eye-catching and these types tend to have a long-lasting quality about them. They are also usually sweetly fragrant and this is a real bonus. A bit of extra space is needed for these plants as they can grow to a large size in time but the reward is well worth the effort. There are many hundreds of white varieties that are fairly similar and are usually all from the same breeding lines, so if this variety is not available there are sure to be many more to choose from.

Laeliocattleya 'Chine'

This fabulous hybrid between the two genera of *Laelia* and *Cattleya* is a good example of successful hybridizing. The large blooms are 6 in. (15 cm) across and have a marvelously thick texture and substance to the petals. This quality makes the flowers extremely long-lived, lasting in perfect condition for at least four weeks. Flowers of this size will need some support as the buds grow and open. With several flowers on a head, these can weigh a considerable amount when fully open. So as the buds emerge from the flowering sheath at the top of the pseudobulb, carefully tie the stem to a cane and repeat if necessary as the stem grows and the flowers open.

CYMBIDIUM

The *Cymbidium* is among the most popular orchids in cultivation and has never been out of fashion. The demand for both plants and cut flowers has existed for well over 100 years, ever since the first hybrids were bred and people became fascinated by this genus. It is often referred to as a beginner's orchid because it is so difficult to kill. Equally, however, it is difficult to grow well.

The natural distribution of this genus is from China in the north, across to Japan, throughout the Himalayas, India, down through Thailand, the Malaya Peninsula, and as far south as northern Australia. The habitat is diverse, with plants growing at high altitudes in the Himalayas, tolerant here of cool nights and hot sunny days. There are also tropical rainforest varieties and even some in Australia that prefer hot desert conditions. The species, such as *C. lowianum* and *C. erythrostylum*, can be found growing as large clumps, high above the ground, in the fork of their host tree where the branches provide dappled light and their position gives plenty of drainage. Other species, such as *C. sinensis* and *C. caniculatum*, grow in very dry, arid conditions in Australia, relying on the annual monsoon rain to water them during their growing season. The hard-leaved species, such as *C. aloifolium* found in Thailand and other parts of Asia, can stand full blazing sun. They grow as epiphytes on deciduous trees or rocky outcrops. There is one species, *C. macrorhizon*, that grows terrestrially, has no green vegetative parts, and lives an entirely subterranean life, only sending its flower spike above the soil.

Due to their habit of growing high in trees, many of these species produce long pendent flower spikes which, when the plants are grown in cultivation, are tied upright mainly for convenience and appearance. Other species, such as *C. insigne*, are terrestrial and grow in long grass among rhododendron bushes. They have thus adapted to produce tall, upright flower spikes with the blooms borne in clusters near the top. As the habitat for cymbidiums varies considerably, so does the growth and shape of the plant. Subsequently, there is great variation in shape, size, and color of the blooms.

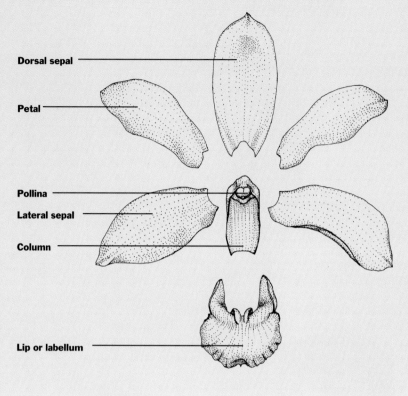

Dorsal sepal

Petal

Pollina

Lateral sepal

Column

Lip or labellum

Above: The *Cymbidium* flower dissected to show all the flower parts.

Miniatures, Compacts, and Standards

Cymbidiums vary considerably in size and are divided into three groups: miniatures, compact growers, and standards. True miniatures will fit into a 4–5 in. (10–12 cm) pot with a flower spike about 18 in. (45 cm) high. They have pretty, petite flowers arranged along the stem. Standard cymbidiums, on the other hand, can grow into very large plants. In huge tubs they will produce magnificent displays of blooms on 48 in. (120 cm) spikes. The compact *Cymbidium* has been produced somewhere between the other two, usually by hybridizing the miniature with the standard. The result is a modern plant which will fit an 7–8 in. (18–20 cm) pot and produce spikes 24–28 in. (60–70 cm) high with four or five spikes on each plant.

A History of Cultivation

Of all the orchids in cultivation, the *Cymbidium* has the longest history. By 2000 B.C., the Chinese and Japanese were cultivating them around their homes and temples for their perfume. *Cymbidium ensifolium*, one of the most strongly scented cymbidiums, comes from southern China and was highly prized. It is still sought after today. The Chinese made no attempt to hybridize from this species but cultivated it just for its perfume. The Japanese have always grown a wide range of miniature *Cymbidium* species, keeping them in very decorative earthenware pots.

Modern European interest in this genus started when the plants were first introduced into England. They became popular for the large conservatories of the Victorians but it wasn't until the end of the nineteenth century that hybridization started. As a result we can enjoy an immense range of colors, shapes and sizes hitherto unimagined by the early growers. By selective breeding it is now possible to produce almost any color except blue.

Hybridization

Surprisingly, only a few species have appeared in our modern hybrids and there are many that have never been bred from at all. As few as five or six species play an important part and only ten or twelve are likely to appear in the background of the hybrids that you will see at any big *Cymbidium* show. This is because the majority have small insignificant flowers and are of less interest to the grower.

By the 1950s, hybridization of cymbidiums had continued at a pace but, as already mentioned, most breeding had been confined to a limited number of species. With the season starting in Europe around February, peaking in March or April, and finishing in May, anyone with early

cymbidiums that bloomed in January was extremely lucky. Flowering before Christmas was almost unheard of but the plants that did were worth their weight in gold.

Selective breeding has now brought the early cymbidiums so far forward that they start blooming as early as July and August and any collector, choosing his plants carefully, can now have cymbidiums in bloom all year round. Most of the hybridizing has been done with the high-altitude species from the Himalayas, with the result that they can be grown anywhere in the world where the temperature is not too high. These hybrids are not suitable for hot tropical lowland climates but do well in Australia, the North Island of New Zealand, South Africa, and California. They are also cultivated throughout Europe.

Providing the Right Conditions

In those parts of the world where the temperature doesn't drop below 50° F (10° C), they can easily be accommodated in shade houses, which provide them with the ideal broken light that they enjoy, or in a greenhouse. Under greenhouse conditions they will flourish, producing many flowers and great rewards to the grower. Their long flower spikes come in an almost unlimited range of colors, shapes, and sizes that will last many weeks in perfection. When the plants are in bloom they

can be successfully brought into the home for all to admire and enjoy. Keep in a cool room in good light, away from a direct source of heat. Straight after flowering they should be returned to the greenhouse where they can continue growing until it is time for the flower spikes to appear again.

In colder climates, such as Europe and the eastern seaboard of the United States, they must be grown in heated greenhouses where the temperature should be maintained at least at 50° F (10° C) on the coldest of winter nights, with a natural rise during the day. These cool nights are essential for the flowering of the plants as in the Himalayas they enjoy very cool nights and hot sunny days.

Some growers prefer to place their cymbidiums out of doors during the frost-free months of the year. They should be placed in a bright, airy position with some broken shade to protect them from the rays of the hot summer sun. Do not put them in a dark corner or behind a thick hedge where no light can reach them. Preferably place them on a raised bench to allow air movement around the plant and to make it difficult for unwanted pests to make their home in the pot.

These plants do not make ideal houseplants in a centrally heated room as the temperature is usually too high at night and the light too poor. This will result in the plant becoming lank, poorly grown, and unlikely to flower.

Day-to-day Care

Cymbidiums should be watered all the year round whether they are indoors or out. Those that are outside for the summer will need extra special care and attention to make sure that on hot sunny days they do not become dehydrated. Cymbidiums will take fertilizer with their water almost all year round, but be more careful in the darkest winter months. They will need most in spring and summer. Whether the plants are indoors or out, by late summer the flower spikes will begin to appear. Great care must be taken to ensure that these spikes are not damaged or eaten by slugs or snails. Once the spike is 6 in. (15 cm) high it will require staking or it will grow at an angle and look untidy. Tie it to a bamboo cane as it grows to ensure it looks at its best. These spikes will grow fast during the late summer and early autumn, but as winter approaches development will slow. The late spring-flowering varieties will almost stand still during the winter and then grow again with the increasing daylight of the spring months. Midwinter-flowering cymbidiums need as much light as possible during the day and cool nighttime temperatures. High temperatures at night combined with poor light levels will result in bud drop.

A new shoot will be produced after flowering that swells to form a new pseudobulb, usually larger than the previous one. Some plants are capable of producing several shoots at a time and, as a result, a mature *Cymbidium* can consist of any number of pseudobulbs, usually 15 or 20. Plants with many pseudobulbs can be divided at the appropriate time, usually immediately after flowering.

Cymbidiums are best grown in a coarse, open soil which their thick, heavy root system will penetrate quickly. Annual repotting is not advisable; every two or three years suits the plants best. They will flower better on their third year when they have become pot bound. There is no limit to the size of pot they can be grown in, but when the plant becomes unmanageable, it should be divided to keep the pot size down. Always allow a minimum of four or five pseudobulbs per plant. Dividing a plant into pieces smaller than

this will result in a drastic reduction in flowering until it has regained a suitable size.

Commercial Cymbidiums

Cymbidiums have always been popular cut flowers, either as single blooms for corsages or made up for wedding bouquets. Their long spikes are also used for large floral displays where their long-lasting qualities have made them popular. In the 1950s they were grown extensively in large beds. This method proved undesirable as roots touching beneath the soil soon spread diseases and viruses throughout the stock. A return to pot culture made the plants more manageable for the grower.

Cymbidiums are also grown in great numbers for the potted plant trade. They are brought to the peak of perfection in bloom and then sold to decorate offices, hotels, and reception rooms. Although today there are fewer amateurs with large greenhouses that can accommodate a sizeable collection of

Above: *Cymbidium erythrostylum.*

Below: *Cymbidium lowianum.*

cymbidiums, their popularity as plants shows no sign of waning. The changing demand and market is being met by the hybridizer producing smaller and more compact plants which more easily fit into the home as potted plants.

There are few genera related to the *Cymbidium* with which it will breed, so the number of intergeneric hybrids is insignificant. Unlike the *Cattleya* and *Odontoglossum* Alliances, where a huge amount of cross-breeding has been done, the *Cymbidium* stands alone.

Cymbidium erythrostylum

This is perhaps one of the prettiest of all the *Cymbidium* species, with an unusual flower shape differing from the normally open style of the *Cymbidium* flower. *C. erythrostylum* has its two upper petals drawn forward over the lip, giving the whole flower an attractive, triangular appearance. The crisp white petals

and sepals and the bold yellow-and-red striped lip are responsible for many white hybrids, especially the more compact varieties. This species is relatively small and is thus ideal for the amateur enthusiast with a cool greenhouse. The graceful spray of up to eight flowers will last for many weeks during the winter. On a mature plant a succession of several spikes may be produced, lengthening the flowering season.

Cymbidium lowianum

This is a stunning species, known for its long, arching spray of large green flowers. This strong coloring, together with the striking deep red bar across the width of the lip, has been used extensively in breeding lines of the modern *Cymbidium* hybrids. It is often quite noticeable where *C. lowianum* has been used, as the shape and coloring is still evident after many generations. The species comes from Thailand and Burma and can be found growing at high altitudes in the trees with its

graceful flower spikes hanging down from the branches. It is still a sought-after species and is grown easily alongside the modern hybrids in a cool greenhouse. The long-lasting flowers will continue for many weeks throughout the spring.

Cymbidium traceyanum

The characteristic striped petals in coffee and green, with the contrasting spotted cream lip, make this another very popular species for use in breeding. The large flowers are held on a tall, arching spray arising from what can be quite a large plant when mature, reaching over 3 ft. (1m) in height. A certain amount of space is needed to accommodate this Thai orchid but it is well worth it just for the unusual fragrance that the flowers produce when they bloom in the autumn. It is an easy orchid to cultivate, enjoying similar conditions to the cool-growing *Cymbidium* hybrids, especially when placed out of doors in the summer. Any modern variety that you see now with some striping in the petals is likely to contain *C. traceyanum* in its family tree.

Cymbidium Cotil Point

There are many standard *Cymbidium* varieties, as well as the miniatures, and these can reach 4½ ft. (1.5m) in height when in full flower, giving a spectacular show with their blooms measuring up to 5 in. (12 cm) across. This subtle rosy-pink hybrid is typical of modern breeding and the most popular types grown today. No difference in culture is needed for these plants, although a little more space is needed to accommodate their larger pseudobulbs and long, strap-like leaves. If you have the space available to grow these types on to mature specimens, they will give you an excellent show of flowers during the late winter and spring.

Above left:
Cymbidium 'Cotil Point'.

Above right:
Cymbidium 'Kiwi Sunrise'.

Below left:
Cymbidium traceyanum.

Below right:
Cymbidium 'Summer Pearl'.

Cymbidium 'Kiwi Sunrise'

Some of the most popular of the miniature cymbidiums are the summer flowering varieties. 'Kiwi Sunrise', bred in New Zealand, is also known for its light fragrance. Evenly spaced flowers on an upright spike make the plant excellent for use in displays, either in the home or greenhouse.

Cymbidium 'Summer Pearl'

Now almost every conceivable flower color is available in the cymbidiums and this is seen to full effect within the miniature or compact hybrids. These plants can still reach 2 ft. (60 cm) in height but this is a lot shorter than some of their standard variety cousins. The flowers are also a lot smaller at around 2 in. (5 cm) across. 'Summer Pearl' is a beautiful pastel cream variety that is typical of the popular and easy-to-grow types available today. It flowers in late summer to autumn and lasts six to eight weeks in bloom, making it an ideal gift. It will grow well and reflower the following year as long as it is kept in a cool and light position.

DENDROBIUM

Among the orchid family there are some huge genera and the dendrobiums are a good example. There are so many different species, sub-species, and divisions that it is uncertain exactly how many dendrobiums there are. New species are constantly being discovered in remote parts of the world, but it is fair to say that there must be about 1,000 different species of *Dendrobium*.

They originate from as far north as China and India, across to Japan, right the way down through the Malay Peninsula and Philippines, and also Borneo, New Guinea, across Australia and the North Island of New Zealand. They are found in every habitat from sea level to the highest mountains and from dry, arid forest to permanently wet jungle. So diverse is this group of orchids that it is impossible to generalize on the shape and cultivation of these plants.

They all produce slender, leafy pseudobulbs, from ¼ in. (0.5 cm) to 6 ft. (2 m) in length. They are sometimes as thick as a man's arm or can be as thin as a pencil. The flowers show bizarre shapes and great diversity in color and size.

Hybrids

There is a huge range of man-made hybrids, which are very popular, using two or three main groups. First of all, extensive hybridizing has been carried out in Japan and Hawaii with an Indian species, *Dendrobium nobile*. This produces large, long-lasting blooms in a rainbow of colors. The breeding of another type, *D. phalaenopsis*, or *D. bigibbum*, has been mostly carried out in Thailand and Singapore. These orchids make ideal cut flowers and are grown by the acre. The blooms are harvested all the year round and distributed all over the world. The third type that has attracted the interest of the hybridizers is a group of Australian species which are grown and interbred mainly in Australia to meet the ever-increasing demand for houseplants and garden plants, where the climate suits them.

Dendrobiums in the Wild

Nearly all the *Dendrobium* species are epiphytic, growing on trees where their elongated pseudobulbs hang down from their host. Some of the smaller species grow on the extremities of trees and bushes where they are known as twig epiphytes. In such precarious positions their life can only be short, as they are easily displaced during storms. Once this has happened and they end up on the ground, their chances of survival are greatly diminished. Because of this risk, these small plants grow quickly to maturity and seed production.

Care and Cultivation

The *Dendrobium* has always been popular; in greenhouses they can be cultivated in quite small pots in coarse, chunky bark or they can be mounted on rafts of tree fern or cork bark and suspended from the roof. Keep regularly sprayed during the growing season to ensure rapid completion of their long, slender pseudobulbs. In the autumn many of the species will lose their leaves and remain deciduous throughout our winter, which corresponds to the dry season in their natural environment. While resting at low temperatures of 45–50° F (8–10° C), these orchids will enjoy all the light that you can give them during dull winters. In the spring each eye, where the foliage has fallen, will produce a flower bud. Some of these orchids produce a dazzling display of blooms, which although short-lived, will be ample reward for the year's care.

Few dendrobiums are continuously growing so they all experience two seasons, with a short, fast growing season when they require plenty of heat, water, and fertilizer. At the end of the growing season they start to rest; some will lose part of their foliage and some will remain evergreen. Whatever the type, it is important that when the season's growth is complete, the water should be withheld. Plants that are watered while resting face the danger of losing their dormant root system or suffering damage to the eyes at the base of the plant; this in turn will upset future growth as the potential flower buds along the stem will produce small plantlets, known as "keikis", instead of flowers. This can be fine if you wish to increase your stock by propagation, but an eye that has produced a surplus growth in this manner will not flower. To prevent the keikis from growing, the plants must be kept dry in winter.

Uses and Abuses

The demand for dendrobiums in Europe has always been present among the cut flower trade, enthusiastic amateurs and the potted plant trade. In the Far East and the United States the demand is enormous, mainly as interior decoration. The idea is to buy the plant in bud, enjoy it for a few weeks while in flower and then throw it away. This sounds like an extravagant waste, but to the commercial nurseries it is simply meeting a market for which there is an insatiable demand.

Dendrobium nobile var. *virginale*

This Himalayan species is an albino form of the more commonly seen pink and purple species. The pure white blooms have no yellow at all in the flower, which is quite

unusual. It flowers remarkably freely in the spring, the clusters of blooms lasting for several weeks. The cooler the plant is kept during the winter and throughout the flowering time, the better and longer lasting the flowers will be.

Dendrobium infundibulum

Many dendrobiums are found in the Himalayan mountain range and this is just one of them. Its strong, tall pseudobulbs are very distinctive as they are covered in a layer of very dark, almost black, hairs. The large, crisp white blooms are very showy and extremely long-lasting, staying perfect for many weeks then turning slightly translucent but still staying on the plant for several more weeks before dropping. Like many of the Himalayan dendrobiums, this is a cool-growing orchid, originating from high altitude habitats.

Above:
Dendrobium nobile var. *virginale*.

Left:
Dendrobium infundibulum.

Dendrobium 'Brownie'

Warm-growing dendrobiums are another group, the species of which originate from the Far East. While most of these types of dendrobium are in the pink and white spectrum, there are some new colors coming along in yellow and green tones, as well as this really unusual coppery-brown which is quite different to the rest of the group. The culture is just the same though, and it will grow happily alongside the other warmth-loving varieties.

Dendrobium 'Emma White'

Warm-growing dendrobiums produce a spray of showy flowers from the top of the most mature pseudobulb, and they can even flower again a second year from the same growth. They come in a wide range of colors but one of the most popular is pure white, a clean and crisp flower that lasts for many weeks on a tall, upright spray.

Dendrobium 'Pink Beauty'

There has been extensive hybridizing with the species D. nobile and its

varieties and related species to produce a host of larger and more colorful hybrids ideal for the cool greenhouse. These plants are now available in every shade of pink and purple, white, and yellow with contrasting patterning and borders. The secret to growing these plants successfully is to give them a cool, light, and dry rest in the winter to encourage the flowers to come in spring.

Dendrobium 'Thai Fancy'

Some warm-growing hybrids, including this variety, have been bred to be more compact in size. It will only reach around 12 in. (30 cm) in height when in flower; compare this with the taller types that can be twice that size. This orchid needs good light and warmth to help flowering so it makes an ideal houseplant for a warm, sunny window sill. A little shade from the brightest summer sun is all that is required. Take care not to keep these types of dendrobium too wet; they prefer to be watered only occasionally, letting the soil dry out in between waterings.

Far left: *Dendrobium* 'Brownie'.

Left: *Dendrobium* 'Pink Beauty'.

Above: *Dendrobium* 'Emma White'.

Right: *Dendrobium* 'Thai Fancy'.

MILTONIOPSIS

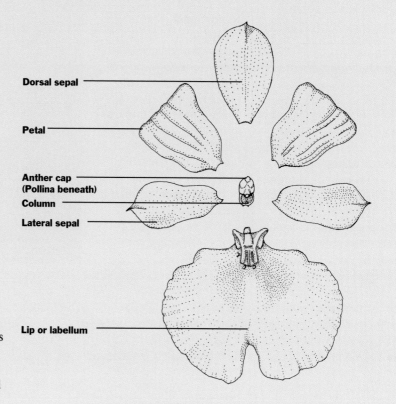

Dorsal sepal

Petal

Anther cap
(Pollina beneath)

Column

Lateral sepal

Lip or labellum

Miltoniopsis are commonly known as the pansy orchids because of their large, flat flowers with their distinctive bold patterning. They are extremely attractive plants to grow. Originally included within the *Odontoglossum* genus, they were then separated into their own genus, *Miltonia*, and more recently divided again into the genus *Miltoniopsis*.

Their wild habitat is restricted to the high cloud forests in the foothills of the Andes in Colombia. There are a limited number of species, such as *M. roezlii*, *M. phalaenopsis*, and *M. vexillaria*. The latter can be found in a range of colors from pure white through shades of pink to a very deep lilac. These three main species have contributed to the enormous range of colors, shapes, and sizes that are available in hybrids today. *M. vexillaria* provides a choice of color and quantity of flowers, up to six or seven on a spike. *M. roezlii* gives shape and splashed petals to the offspring, but reduces the flower count; and *M. phalaenopsis*, with its patterned lip, contributes the waterfall effect on many of the wonderful hybrids. Individually, the perfume is not strong but a house full of *Miltoniopsis* is highly scented as well as being a dazzling sight.

As *Miltoniopsis* is related to the odontoglossums, the intergeneric hybrids between these two are common. Here, the older name of *Miltonia* is retained and the hybrids are called *Odontonia*. In cultivation, these plants are best grown in conditions similar to those provided for odontoglossums, but preferably a little warmer. Maintain a minimum nighttime temperature of 60° F (15° C) and protect from strong light, especially

Above: The Miltoniopsis flower dissected to show all the flower parts.

Far right: Miltoniopsis 'Beall's Strawberry Joy'.

on hot summer days; their pale, almost grey-green, leaves are susceptible to light burn.

Related to these plants are the Brazilian miltonias with which they once shared a genus. These hard-leaved plants are equally as beautiful and just as easy to grow given similar conditions.

Miltoniopsis phalaenopsis

Not to be confused with the genus *Phalaenopsis*, this dwarf-growing species is extremely attractive with its white flower heavily patterned with a deep red "waterfall" effect on its lip. This dramatic patterning is highly desirable and any hybrid that displays this trait will have *M. phalaenopsis* in its background. The hybrids are certainly a little easier to cultivate than the original species but if you manage to keep this little gem happy, it can grow into a tidy clump and produce a fine show when in full bloom in late spring.

Miltoniopsis roezlii

Not all the *Miltoniopsis* species have large flowers, in fact most are a lot smaller than the hybrids we are used to seeing. This species is miniature and usually only produces one flower at a time. It is quite striking though; the crisp white petals and sepals and enlarged, rounded lip are highlighted by the yellow mask in the center and two dark crimson "eyes" on either side. *M. roezlii* has been responsible for the white breeding line in these orchids and larger white hybrids often have the same characteristic markings. Due to its small size it can be a challenge to grow well but it is well worth seeking out and giving a try. Like all *Miltoniopsis*, this little one does not like to be too wet, cold or in bright sunlight.

Miltoniopsis vexillaria

This particular species is typical of the pansy orchids and has the largest flowers of all the species that originate from Colombia. The rosy-pink coloring is highly variable and can range from pure white, through a delicate pale shade of pink, to deep rose. The darkest of these have influenced the popular deep maroon modern hybrids. *M. vexillaria* is still a popular species to grow, although the hybrid *Miltoniopsis* are more often seen today. It holds its own easily with its large showy flowers and long-lasting quality. Its summer flowers fill the house with beauty and scent when many of the other orchids are putting their energy into growing.

Miltoniopsis 'Beall's Strawberry Joy'

Here the delicate pink has been enhanced further by the addition of a stunning dark mask in the center. The deep maroon is highlighted by the bright white surround. This variety and other closely related hybrids in a similar color range have proved to be particularly popular. They are tolerant of indoor conditions, enjoying the shade and warmth of the modern home. They do prefer high humidity, though, so regular misting of the foliage and the introduction of other orchids and houseplants in the same area will help to make the plants grow and flower better.

Miltoniopsis 'Eureka'

The large blooms of this white hybrid are typical of the delicate, subtle shades and pastel colors that are present in many of the pansy orchids. The contrasting white of the flower and the bold darker markings in the center really make it stand out. The yellow in the very center is designed to signal to passing insects that this is where they can receive a sweet reward if they visit the flower. This is also helped by its sweet fragrance common among *Miltoniopsis* varieties. The scent is enhanced on sunny summer days when the plants are in bloom.

Miltoniopsis 'Jersey'

The deep crimson shade of this fabulous variety is a far step from the pink species, but years of selective breeding have made the resulting blooms dark and velvety. The paler outline and mask set off the bloom well and it is guaranteed to give an excellent show either in the home or in the heated greenhouse. These orchids are mainly summer flowering, ensuring a great show when many orchids are putting their efforts into growing instead.

Left:
Miltoniopsis 'Jersey'.

Above:
Miltoniopsis 'Eureka'.

Right:
Miltoniopsis vexillaria.

83

ODONTOGLOSSUM ALLIANCE

The *Odontoglossum* Alliance is a huge group of orchids, at the center of which is the genus *Odontoglossum*. These plants will readily interbreed with many other closely related genera, producing some of the most complex hybrids in the orchid kingdom. Sometimes up to seven or eight different genera have been involved in producing a hybrid unlike any naturally occurring species. Oncidiums and miltonias are some of the plants most readily hybridized, but these are classified under their own heading as they produce many fascinating hybrids within their own groups. Odontoglossums and their related genera are widespread throughout Central and South America. They are mostly high-altitude plants, requiring cool conditions, from the Andes, crossing the Panama Isthmus, and as far north as Mexico. Recent taxonomic changes within these closely related plants have resulted in many of the families being split up with the creation of new genera. For example, all the former odontoglossums that came from Guatemala and Mexico have now been regrouped as *Lemboglossum*, *Rossioglossum*, and so on, leaving only the plants found in the Andes, mostly from Colombia and Ecuador, in the genus *Odontoglossum*.

The area from which these orchids originate is cool cloud forest, which, although close to the equator, is never too hot during the day and always cool at night. These orchids are, therefore, difficult to grow in tropical countries. In Britain, the Victorian growers fell in love with the odontoglossums and called them the queen of orchids. At one time they were being imported at a rate of 100,000 plants each year, many of which perished on the long sea journey from South America, or failed through lack of understanding in overheated Victorian greenhouses.

Odontoglossum crispum fascinated them the most as it came in several hundred different varieties, from pure white to heavily spotted yellow and maroon flowers. Because of the inaccessibility of the high valleys in which these orchids grew, each variety had evolved separately in its own isolated environment.

As well as *O. crispum*, *O. pescatorei*, *O. hallii*, and *O. triumphans* were among the orchids that were available in unlimited quantities at the turn of the century. The over-collecting of these plants led to their near extinction in the wild and, sadly, very few of them are to be found in cultivation today.

The Hybrids

The greatest demand is for *Odontoglossum* hybrids that have been crossed with related genera such as miltonias, oncidiums, and cochliodas which not only increase the range of color, shape, and size but give a more vigorous plant. When two genera are crossed together, such as *Odontoglossum* and *Cochlioda*, the two names are used to produce the name for the new plants, in this case the resulting hybrids are called *Odontioda*. When such a hybrid is crossed with another genera, for example *Miltonia*, the new plants are named after the breeder, in this case *Vuylstekeara*, named after Charles Vuylsteke. All intergeneric hybrids arising from three or more natural genera are named after a person in this way.

The introduction of *Brassia* or *Oncidium* into the blood of such hybrids will make the resulting plants more heat tolerant, which means that some of them can be grown in Florida and other places which would normally be too warm for the pure odontoglossums.

Cultivation of Odontoglossums

A strong, healthy, mature plant should consist of four to six pseudobulbs with a strong new growth. These orchids do not make enormous specimen plants and will seldom grow at the same time as they flower. Each pseudobulb consists of two basal leaves and one or two terminal leaves from the top, the flower spike coming from the base or side of the pseudobulb. Due to their origins, living in almost perpetual spring-like weather, these orchids know little or no seasonal change and therefore grow continuously without a definite flowering season. In fact, most of these plants will grow and flower on a nine-month cycle, so they seldom bloom at the same time two years running, with the result that a mixed collection of the *Odontoglossum* Alliance will give flowers almost all the year round.

They are best grown in a cool greenhouse with a minimum night-time temperature of 50° F (10° C), with a variable daytime rise depending on the weather. From early spring onwards, the greenhouse should be well shaded to prevent overheating and scorching of the foliage, especially on hot summer days. The floor and staging should be kept constantly moist to provide an even humidity; combine this with fresh air to give a buoyant atmosphere.

Beallara 'Tahoma Glacier Green'

The addition of *Brassia* can be seen clearly in this stunning hybrid with its star-shaped bloom typical of the spider orchids. This plant is relatively heat tolerant and could be grown in a warmer room or greenhouse heated to a minimum of 55° F (12° C) with good light. It is also very versatile and would be equally at home in a cool house that drops a few degrees cooler than this. This particular variety is fantastic with its large flowers measuring up to 4 in. (10cm) across; an individual spray will hold up to eight flowers. It is not unusual for these orchids to make multiple growths and therefore produce a succession of flower spikes over many months.

Left: *Beallara* 'Tahoma Glacier Green'.

Lemboglossum cervantesii

Once part of the *Odontoglossum* genus, this plant is still regarded as such by many people, although it has been reclassified into its own group. This is a small-growing species, not reaching more than 6 in. (15cm) in height. The flowers are quite large in comparison and very striking, up to 2 in. (5cm) across and white, sometimes flushed with light pink, with deep red bands towards the center of the flower. It originates from the high mountains of Mexico so this, together with its dwarf habit, makes it ideal for the mixed cool collection where space is limited. It is perhaps not as widely available as it used to be, but is certainly worth seeking out.

Odontioda 'Garnet'

Virtually every flower color is present in the *Odontoglossum* Alliance and the reds were among the first to be bred. The inclusion of the genus *Cochlioda*, and especially the species *Cochlioda noetzliana*, revolutionized the red breeding in these orchids. Now there are many different red varieties, all of which tend to be quite easy to grow. Their strong colors and tolerance of high temperatures and light make these among the most popular orchids for beginners.

Left:
Lemboglossum cervantesii.

Above:
Odontoglossum hallii.

Below: *Odontioda 'Garnet'.*

Right: *Vuylstekeara 'Cambria Plush' FCC/RHS.*

Far right: *Odontoglossum 'Geyser Gold'.*

Odontoglossum hallii

This *Odontoglossum* species comes from Ecuador where it grows at high altitude and lives in quite cool conditions. This makes it an ideal plant to grow in the cool greenhouse where the temperature does not drop below 50° F (10° C). The robust plant produces pale green leaves and an arching spray of large yellow flowers, spotted with dark chocolate brown. This species is strongly fragrant, something of a real bonus rarely found among the odontoglossums. It flowers freely in the summer months, the flowers lasting for around four to six weeks in cool conditions. This is certainly a widely grown orchid and is fairly easy to obtain.

Vuylstekeara 'Cambria Plush' FCC/RHS
This is perhaps one of the best known *Odontoglossum* Alliance hybrids produced in the twentieth century, which is still being produced in large quantities today. The three different genera of *Miltonia, Odontoglossum,* and *Cochlioda* were crossed together to form this complex but highly desirable plant. The bold red petals and sepals contrast well with the bright white lip, also spotted in rich burgundy red. Mature plants can produce a tall spray of these large flowers twice a year. The flowers will last four to six weeks in full bloom. Due to complex breeding, this hybrid is more heat-tolerant than some of the other plants in the group so it is a good variety to grow in the home where conditions are a little warmer.

Odontoglossum 'Geyser Gold'
This brightly colored hybrid is unusual with its totally yellow flowers, comprising dark yellow spotting on a pale yellow background. This coloring has been made possible by the use of a completely yellow variety of the species, *O. bictoniense,* as one of the parents, which is itself quite rare.

Mature plants will produce tall spikes with up to ten flowers, often with two flower spikes per pseudobulb. It is quite tolerant of cooler temperatures so will grow well with other orchids that will withstand a drop in temperature to 50° F (10° C) or even slightly below.

ONCIDIUM ALLIANCE

Oncidium was a huge genus with many closely related species but is another that has been subjected to taxonomic revision, resulting in many oncidiums being reclassified. They still remain close to the original *Oncidium* group and so are referred to collectively as the *Oncidium* Alliance. They readily interbreed with closely related genera such as *Miltonia* and *Odontoglossum*, which produce complex, interesting offspring.

Members of the Alliance are very widely distributed throughout South America, except in the extreme south and the deserts. They can be found from sea level to the high altitude cloud forests of the Andes, throughout Central America as far north as Mexico, and on the islands of the West Indies. As there are both high and low altitude plants, they can be cultivated almost anywhere in the world. For example, large quantities are grown in Thailand and Singapore for the cut flower trade although this is not their original home. The bright golden oncidiums are very popular and will grow equally well as potted plants or cut flowers.

Growth habits vary considerably, from robust pseudobulbs on long extended rhizomes climbing in rainforest trees, to very small, dainty plants which only grow on the slender branches and leaves. The latter are called twig epiphytes. By their very nature they are short-lived, easily falling from their host tree at the time of hurricanes or strong winds. They quickly reproduce from seed to ensure survival of the species.

These small species belong to a group known as "equitant oncidiums" and are best grown on pieces of cork bark or in very small clay pots where they thrive on high humidity and bright sunshine.

Certain cool-growing oncidiums from Mexico, such as *Oncidium tigrinum* and *O. incurvum*, hybridize readily with the South American *Odontoglossum* species, resulting in some beautiful odontocidiums with their long sprays of highly colored flowers. Because of the diversity within the *Oncidium* genus, it is not possible to hybridize between all the different species; most of them prefer to breed with their closely related cousins.

Oncidium 'Boissiense'
This is just one of many popular and easy-to-grow "golden shower" oncidiums. The showy hybrids from species such as this produce tall, branching flower spikes that can reach 24 in. (60 cm) or more and hold hundreds of flowers. Their small, golden-yellow blooms give a spectacular show en masse and are very long-lasting. So much so that they are used extensively as cut blooms around the world. These types of *Oncidium* are extremely versatile and will often grow well in both cool and warm conditions with plenty of light all the year round, although not direct summer sun.

Oncidium cheirophorum
This is one of the smallest-growing of the oncidiums and originates in Colombia. Its dwarf habit makes it ideal to fit in a corner of the cool house or even grow in an indoor orchid tank. It will never reach more than about 3 in. (8 cm) in height and the tiny flowers are only ½ in. (1 cm) across. The dainty little flowers are held on a branched, arching spray; often several sprays are produced from a pseudobulb. The flowers are the brightest of yellows with no contrasting markings. They also give off a very strong fragrance for such little flowers. They flower mainly in autumn on completion of the season's pseudobulbs.

Right: *Oncidium cheirophorum.*

Far right: *Oncidium 'Boissiense'.*

Left: *Oncidium maculatum.*

Below: *Oncidium ornithorhynchum.*

Right top: *Oncidium tigrinum* var. *unguiculatum.*

Right bottom: *Oncidium* 'Sharry Baby Sweet Fragrance'.

Oncidium maculatum

This plant has a strong, robust habit. The slightly ridged pseudobulbs have a pair of dark green leaves and the flower spikes are produced in autumn and winter. The graceful stem can be arching and even branched in mature specimens, with many flowers along its length. The flowers are around 1 in. (3 cm) across on a stem that can reach 20 in. (50 cm) in height. The petals and sepals are green with brown spotting and the narrow lip is a pale cream. This species is also strongly scented. It makes an easy orchid to cultivate and is free flowering when grown in cool conditions and in dappled light in summer.

Oncidium ornithorhynchum

If you have restricted space either in a cool greenhouse or on a shady window sill then this orchid will do well in either position. Unusually for oncidiums, this one is pink in color. It is also very showy, producing many stems of dainty little flowers at one time, usually during the autumn. The charming rosy blooms also have a very strong, sweet scent. It is an ideal orchid for beginners, being easy to grow, and is extremely free flowering while staying compact and easy to handle. These plants grow well into maturity when they will produce several flowering stems per pseudobulb.

Oncidium tigrinum var. unguiculatum

Many of the *Oncidium* species are yellow in color and this particular one is typical of the type. Its showy flowers are held on a tall, upright stem and the chocolate brown, blotched petals and sepals contrast vividly with the large, bright golden-yellow lip. The plant does not grow too large and is quite manageable for the amateur grower to keep in a cool orchid house. It has been used frequently in many *Oncidium* breeding lines to enhance the golden yellow coloring seen in the hybrids.

Oncidium 'Sharry Baby Sweet Fragrance'

The species *O. ornitho-rhynchum* has been used in the breeding of this very popular and attractive hybrid and this is what gives it its strong chocolate scent as well as its deep maroon coloring. The tall branching flower sprays will take a few weeks to reach their full height but when they do, the numerous flowers will last for many weeks, especially when kept in a cool position. While growing, this orchid will be tolerant of both cool and slightly warmer temperatures, requiring a minimum temperature of 50–55° F (10–12° C) in winter. It also needs fairly good light to encourage flowering for the following year.

PAPHIOPEDILUM, PHRAGMIPEDIUM, & CYPRIPEDIUM

These are three distinct genera of orchids that must have come from a common ancestry but are now so distantly related that, although they look and grow alike and have much in common with each other, never interbreed. Cypripediums and paphiopedilums are very popular orchids in cultivation and those who grow one genus also grow the other. They are successful growing in the same conditions, although they come from totally different parts of the world and would never meet in nature. The cypripediums are the common link between the other two genera and are circumboreal, meaning they are found all around the top of the globe from the Arctic Circle downwards, across the American continent, Europe, and Asia. They are opportunist plants when growing in extremely cold regions, with a short, fast growing season between the long periods of cold. Paphiopedilums are found from southern China, through India, Thailand, the Malay Peninsula, and on the many islands of South East Asia. Some of the most spectacular species come from Borneo and Sarawak. Phragmipediums, on the other hand, are from central South America. Some of the finest varieties are high-altitude plants from the Andes.

All three genera conform to the same habit of growth, producing a creeping rhizome with each season's growth and a series of thick, fleshy leaves. The flower spike is always produced from the center of the latest growth and can bear one or many flowers. The blooms are some of the most striking and unique in the orchid kingdom. The lip has evolved into a pouch, which attracts and catches insects merely for pollination, not for food as orchids are not insectivorous. The shoe-shaped pouch has earned these plants the common name of slipper orchid. They are sometimes also known as the virgin's slipper and the Canadian species is called the moccasin flower by the native people.

Paphiopedilum

An interest in the paphiopedilums has existed since the beginning of orchid cultivation. Particular favorites were the cool-growing, high-altitude species from the Himalayas, namely *Paphiopedilum insigne*, *P. spicerianum*, *P. villosum*, and *P. fairrieanum*. These orchids were grown in huge quantities for the cut flower trade. Unfortunately, the fashion has changed, but potted plants have come to the fore instead.

The natural habitat of these species can range from rocky outcrops on limestone cliffs to places high up in the trees, where huge clumps can grow as epiphytes. The spectacular, multi-flowering species from Borneo are somewhat slow-growing but when they do bloom the reward is well worth the wait. This especially applies to *P. rothschildianum* and *P. sanderianum*.

The genus has always been collected by growers and hybridization has produced some wonderful and striking new flowers only hinted at in the original species. Amazingly, new species are still being discovered and in the last 20 years there has hardly been a year when a new surprise has not come from an unknown quarter. Many new species have come from China, north Vietnam, and Laos. Hybridizers are beginning to work with these exciting new shapes and colors and have amazed the orchid world. Species such as *P. malipoense* with its tall, slender stem and pale green flowers, *P. macranthum* with the largest pouch and bright pink coloring, and *P. armeniacum* with its dazzling golden yellow blooms, have all done so much to widen our knowledge of the South East Asian slipper orchids.

Phragmipediums

Phragmipediums from central South America can be found either as epiphytes on trees or growing on rocks overhanging river banks. The tallest of them is *Phragmipedium longifolium* whose spike can reach 4½ ft. (1.5 m), producing a continuous display of flowers but never more than two or three on a stem at any one time. As the old flower drops off so the new one will open and in this manner some spikes will continue to bear flowers for two years. A large specimen plant will be sending up new spikes all the time with the result that the plant is never out of bloom.

In England, the Victorians experimented with hybridizing in this group and produced several very interesting plants, but because the range of species and colors is limited compared with the paphiopedilums, they are mostly pale green and brown, with the odd exception producing pink blooms. The main attraction for the grower is the long, thin, ribbon-like petals, hanging down on each side of the bloom, especially in *P. caudatum* which has the longest petals of all.

After early experiments in hybridizing, performed without any knowledge of genetics, it was found that the offspring were sterile and from then on all breeding ceased. In the last 20 years of the twentieth century, however, a new interest was kindled in these plants for two reasons. First, the discovery of a new species high up in the Andes called *P. besseae*, which produces brilliant red flowers, a color totally unimagined in this group of pastel orchids. Secondly, a better understanding of genetics and the ability to adapt those plants that were unable to breed. The result is that *Phragmipedium* breeding has taken off at a pace, crossing *P. besseae* with all the other known species to produce a whole new range of shapes, sizes, and colors, from dark pinks and reds to deep burgundy.

Culture

The culture of cypripediums is exceedingly slow and is only for a person prepared to accept a challenge. Being such cold-growing plants, if grown under glass they should be in an alpine house maintained at just frost-free temperatures. When they are cultivated, usually in herbaceous borders, they are capable of eventually making large clumps. Paphiopedilums and phragmipediums will grow well in a similar set-up with a minimum temperature of about 60° F (15° C) on the coldest of winter nights. The plants should always be shaded from direct sunlight and be kept evenly moist all the year round. The paphiopedilums will grow well in a bark or bark and peat mix, whereas phragmipediums seem to do very well in rockwool, as they like permanent moisture.

Above:
Paphiopedilum
'Chiquita'.

Paphiopedilum chamberlainianum

This warm-growing *Paphiopedilum* prefers to be kept at a minimum of 60° F (15° C) in winter. It is one of a small group of species that flower sequentially. The flower spike first produces one flower but then, as this starts to fade, the next bud further up the stem starts to open. This continues for many months until the final bud has been produced, adding up to about eight throughout the year. The individual flowers are quite showy; the pouched lip is a brilliant magenta pink with darker, greenish-brown petals at the sides. The dorsal sepal above has bold purple striping against a white and green background. Not always widely available, but when grown this plant is quite easily cultivated either indoors or in a warm greenhouse.

Paphiopedilum insigne

This slipper orchid is one of a group of cool-growing paphiopedilums that are very much at home in a cool greenhouse alongside such orchids as cymbidiums and pleiones. Since Victorian times, it has been traditionally grown as a potted plant, flowering for many weeks over winter with handsome copper-colored flowers. The blooms are produced singly, but on plants of a considerable size the high yield of flowers can provide a stunning show. This species used to be grown extensively for cut flowers, showing just how long the flowers last. A cool, shady, and moist environment is just right for these orchids and they are easily obtainable and well worth growing.

Above left:
Paphiopedilum insigne.

Above right:
Paphiopedilum 'Helvetia'.

Below left:
Paphiopedilum spicerianum.

Far right top:
Paphiopedilum 'Lebaudyanum'.

Far right bottom:
Paphiopedilum 'Maudiae'.

Paphiopedilum spicerianum

This is another of the cool-growing paphiopedilums and all of this group have plain green leaves. Many of the warm-growing types have highly patterned, mottled foliage. This plant will grow easily into a tidy clump of leaves and as it increases in size and produces more new shoots each year, so the number of flowers will increase too. The flowers are dominated by the white dorsal petal, dramatically striped down the center with dark purple. The rest of the flower is a browny-green, the petals at the side having a wavy edge and a purple stripe too. This species will also flower through autumn and winter, growing well alongside *P. insigne*.

Paphiopedilum 'Helvetia'

There are many primary hybrids still in cultivation today that were first crossed over 100 years ago. *P.* 'Helvetia' is one such plant, a cross between the species *P. philippinense* and *P. chamberlainianum*. It produces several flowers, all open at once, a characteristic derived from *P. philippinense*. Its pink tinging on the yellow flower comes from the other parent. These plants will continue to produce a few more buds at the tip of the stem, making them last even longer in flower. Like many of these orchids, the plants will stay compact and will not take up much space in the warm section of a greenhouse, enjoying the shade provided by other taller orchids around them.

Paphiopedilum 'Maudiae'

Some of the boldest *Paphiopedilum* hybrids have been these green and white varieties. The pure, translucent coloring is unique and, teamed with the striking white-and-green striped dorsal sepal, these are always popular. The single flowers can be quite large on some of the related hybrids, up to 4 in. (10 cm) across and on a stem 12 in. (30 cm) high. These flowers are also very long-lasting and will cut well too.

Another characteristic is the highly mottled leaves that have a pale green background overlaid with deep green patches and blotches. This means that even when out of flower these plants look very attractive. All mottled-leaved paphiopedilums should be kept warm at all times.

Phragmipedium besseae

This species is a relative newcomer on the orchid scene and it has opened up a whole range of new colors and hybridizing prospects for this group of orchids. This plant was recently discovered in Peru and Ecuador, and the brilliant red color of the flower makes it a real winner. The various shades of red and orange that have followed in its hybrids are bringing this plant to everyone's attention the world over. As a species it is a bit of a challenge to grow well, but the hybrids are proving to be fast to produce and they grow easily in a warm, moist, and shady position alongside paphiopedilums and phalaenopsis. As with all the phragmipediums, this one flowers sequentially, lasting for many weeks as one opening bud follows the previous falling flower.

Paphiopedilum 'Lebaudyanum'

This is a very old primary hybrid between *P. haynaldianum* and *P. philippinense*, which is still much sought after today, although not always widely available. It grows into quite a large plant with plenty of long, plain green leaves. The flower spike produces multiple flowers that all open at the same time rather than producing them in succession like some other multi-flowering paphiopedilums.

Phragmipedium longifolium

These orchids are terrestrial so they are not restricted by size, as they do not have the risk of falling out of a tree. This species certainly needs space to grow: as the name suggests it has very long, thick leaves that will grow upwards until their weight causes them to bend over. The flower spike is even taller, reaching 6 ft. (2 m) quite easily. The flower spike will continue to grow, constantly producing further buds at its tip and even sometimes branching off. The flowers themselves do not last that long but the succession of blooms means that mature specimens can be in flower for well over 18 months. They are worth growing if you have the space and the warmth to do so.

Phragmipedium pearcei

While some *Phragmipedium* species can be quite large, this one is a miniature among giants. The flower spikes reach only 4–6 in. (10–15 cm) high, just above the thin, dark green leaves. The flowers have a pale green background overlaid with darker striping, with long, twisted petals hanging at the sides. The plant has an elongated rhizome between each new growth, giving it a creeping habit that fills a small pot quite quickly. The plant easily expands into a clump that will produce several flower spikes at once. This is a fairly strong species, despite its size, and well worth including if you would like to try this family but are short on space.

Above:
Phragmipedium longifolium.

Right:
Phragmipedium pearcei.

Below:
Phragmipedium 'Hanne Popow'.

Far right top:
Phragmipedium 'Longueville'.

Far right bottom:
Phragmipedium 'Sorcerer's Apprentice'.

Phragmipedium 'Hanne Popow'

This is a fairly recent *Phragmipedium* hybrid from the pink species *P. schlimii*, popular as it introduces a different color range into the family. The rosy-pink blushing on the petals and sepals goes well with the deeper pink, round, pouched lip.

Phragmipedium 'Longueville'

This is one of the new generation of *P. besseae* hybrids, and really shows a wonderful shade of pinkish-orange that has been passed down to this hybrid. The plant is certainly stronger than *P. besseae*, which is usually the case, as seedlings end up with a certain amount of hybrid vigor. The flowers have wonderful shape and substance. They will last several weeks before dropping and many more will be produced on the flower stem.

Phragmipedium 'Sorcerer's Apprentice'

A hybrid arising from *P. longifolium*, this too can be a large plant but not to quite the same extent. The flowers are a shiny copper color around the pouch, with speckled green inside, and pink-edged green petals and sepals. The plant has the same ability as its parent to make more buds at the tip of the flower spike, so flowers for months and months at a time. Again, this needs to be kept in warm, shady, and moist conditions. A peculiarity of these orchids is that the flowers do not tend to show any signs of fading, but simply drop from the stem when spent, even though they still appear to be in perfect condition. This can be a worrying time for the uninitiated but it is perfectly normal.

PHALAENOPSIS

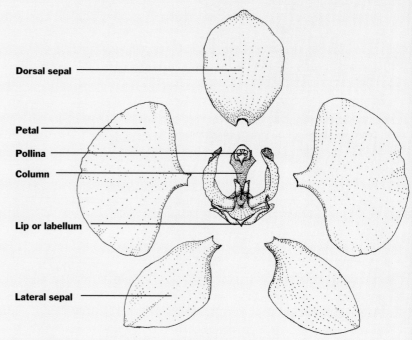

Dorsal sepal

Petal

Pollina

Column

Lip or labellum

Lateral sepal

Above: The *Phalaenopsis* flower dissected to show all the flower parts.

More *Phalaenopsis* plants are raised than any other genus. The huge increase in their popularity has been brought about by the great interest in orchids as houseplants. Their long-lasting qualities and their ease to settle into centrally heated homes makes them ideal subjects.

Throughout the world there are many nurseries totally devoted to this orchid, where the plants are not counted in hundreds or thousands but in the acreage of greenhouses in which they are grown. It is not unusual to find several nurseries covering five or more acres devoted only to the production of this orchid.

This genus is distributed throughout tropical South East Asia, with the most important species occurring in the Philippines, Borneo, and Malaya. Some can be found as far away as Burma and India. These tropical lowland orchids grow as epiphytes in warm, moist conditions, in climates that have little or no dry season, so they continuously grow and consequently, continuously flower. They know no real seasonal changes.

The plants are monopodial; the roots, which appear from the base of the plant, climb profusely over the host tree, acting as a firm anchor. The flower spikes are produced from the side in between the leaves and the plant tends to hang down from its host, with long flower spikes, sometimes as much as 3 ft. (1 m) in length. The flowers last many weeks and present a dazzling sight when grown as a tropical garden plant.

Many species have intricately mottled foliage, making them even more desirable. This feature has been neglected by the hybridizers, so most plants available commercially have plain leaves. The flowers of different species vary considerably from small, pale pink blooms in *Phalaenopsis equestris*, produced in succession from a continuously flowering spike, to a single-flowered stem in *P. violacea* where no more than one or two blooms are open at any one time. The large, glistening white *P. amabilis* is stunning. The long sprays last for many months in perfection. Related are other whites that have patterned petals, such as *P. stuartiana*. There are also pinks in various shades, including *P. schilleriana* and *P. sanderiana*.

Hybridizing from these species was never popular and throughout most of the twentieth century, little or no breeding was done; most nurseries carried just a few plants in stock. From the late 1970s, however, interest in orchids as houseplants increased and it became apparent that *Phalaenopsis*, although tropical plants, were at home with central heating.

Successful Cultivation

The plant is intolerant of both low temperatures (below 65° F (18° C)) and very high temperatures. So the centrally heated room kept at a constant temperature with poor natural light, although unsuitable for most houseplants, can provide ideal conditions for *Phalaenopsis*, provided they are watered and fed regularly. They will give an

almost perpetual display of flowers. There are records of plants never out of bloom for two or three years, although these are the exception.

In their natural habitat, they experience very little seasonal change. The position in the home is very important for the long-term success of this plant. If placed on a bright, sunny window sill close to the glass, the heat from the sun is likely to scorch the leaves and do severe damage to the plant. Equally, if placed in the darkest corner of the room, the plant will not get sufficient light to make it grow and flower as it should. A well-lit position, without direct light, preferably with a net curtain between the plant and the glass, will ensure that it receives the right amount of dappled sunlight to encourage it to flower freely. Keep the orchid evenly moist all year, checking it at least once a week to make sure it is not too wet or too dry. Due to its epiphytic nature, the plant does not like to stand permanently in water; this will rot the roots quickly. A little fertilizer added to the water on a weekly basis and poured in from the top will be sufficient to keep the plant fit and healthy.

Between the base of the flower spike and the first bloom are a number of eyes on the stem, usually three or four. When the orchid has finished flowering, the stem can be cut back to one of these eyes. Choose the fattest, strongest eye and cut the stem about ½ in. (1 cm) above it. Nine times out of ten, this eye will branch and produce a fresh display of flowers within a few months. If the flowers have withered and dropped off and the stem has started to die back, however, the chances of producing a new flower spike become slimmer. In either case, if the old flower spike is cut off right to the base, next to the plant, no harm is done. The orchid will, very soon, send a new spike from the opposite side of the plant, which will produce flowers within a few months.

Very occasionally, growers may experience difficulty in getting their *Phalaenopsis* to flower in this way. If this happens, yet the plant is strong, growing well, and making new roots, its position should be changed to either a brighter or cooler room. Remember that every room is a microclimate and placing the orchid in a slighter cooler place may encourage it to flower.

Hybrids

From the handful of species already discussed, a rainbow of colors, shapes and sizes has arisen. It is possible to have plants in many colors from yellows, reds, and pinks to purples and whites, and a range of spotted and patterned blooms varying in size, on either single or branched stems. Being monopodial, the *Phalaenopsis* are closely related to many other genera with which, in theory, they should breed readily. However, the partner most commonly used for crossing is *Doritis*, a genus of orchids from Malaya, particularly *Doritis pulcherrima*. This has introduced a much darker, different-shaped flower, but with so much back-crossing some *Doritaenopsis* bear no resemblance to the original species. *Phalaenopsis* will also cross with vandas, aerides, and numerous other monopodials but this has not proved very successful. The vast majority of work has been done within the genus itself.

Once the hybridizer has produced new colors, shapes, and sizes, the plants are then propagated by tissue culture using one of the eyes on the flower spike and the customer buying their orchids from a nursery will have a choice of seedlings or tissue culture stock. These are the two methods by which the plants are readily propagated. Their monopodial habit makes them impossible to propagate by any other method; unlike bulbous orchids, they cannot be divided.

Right: *Phalaenopsis amabilis* is one of the common ancestors of many of today's modern white hybrids.

Pests and Diseases

Orchids grown as houseplants are effectively living in a desert, free from any pests and diseases. They will remain so unless something is introduced. Once a pest, free from natural predators in the home, does become established on a *Phalaenopsis*, what has been paradise for the orchid will become paradise for the bugs. Fortunately, there are very few pests that will attack a *Phalaenopsis* although the most serious is mealy bug. Check the undersides of the leaves and the backs of the flowers regularly, as these are the two main places where the bugs like to congregate. This should ensure that it is not allowed to get a hold. The use of insecticides in the home is not recommended; it is better to remove the offending insect with soapy water.

Phalaenopsis amabilis
Like many of the other *Phalaenopsis* species, this one also grows easily in cultivation, either as a greenhouse plant or in the home, enjoying warmth and protection from bright sunshine in the summer. Its large, clear white blooms have been used extensively in the breeding of the popular large, white hybrids that have been improved over many years of hybridizing. Even with all the hybrids available today, this species is still very popular for its compact and free-flowering habit.

Phalaenopsis equestris

Phalaenopsis equestris is certainly the smallest of all the *Phalaenopsis* species and this really adds to its charm. This orchid comes from the Philippines and the dainty rose-pink and white flowers measure no more than 1 in. (2 cm) across. The branching flower spikes bear many flowers together, with many additional buds being made all the time, extending the flowering period to months on end. The compact flower stem gives a beautiful display set off against the characteristic dark green, glossy leaves. The small size of this lovely species is responsible for many of the new miniature hybrids that are now being produced, making the *Phalaenopsis* family even easier to accommodate.

Far left top:
Phalaenopsis equestris.

Far left bottom:
Phalaenopsis schilleriana.

Above left:
Phalaenopsis 'Bel Croute'.

Above right:
Phalaenopsis 'Cool Breeze'.

Below:
Phalaenopsis 'Penang Girl'.

Phalaenopsis schilleriana
As already mentioned, there are a few species that have attractively patterned leaves as well as beautifully delicate flowers. In the case of *P. schilleriana*, the leaves have a deep green background with silvery grey mottling. It is really the subtle spray of lilac-pink flowers that has been selected for breeding rather than these stunning leaves but occasionally you will see a hybrid with the recognizable patterning in the foliage which indicates its parentage. This species from the Philippines grows well alongside the modern hybrids, needing the same levels of warmth and light, and could be grown as a houseplant with relative ease. These types do not have a strict flowering season so can produce blooms at any time of year, lasting for many weeks at a time.

Phalaenopsis 'Bel Croute'
An avenue of breeding that has become extremely popular in recent years is that from the species *P. equestris*. This charming little miniature, with a host of flowers, has proved to be an excellent ingredient in making compact but very free-flowering plants. *P.* 'Bel Croute' is just one of these, its flowers being only around 1 in. (3 cm) across with a gloriously rich purple coloring. These plants have branching stems so even more flowers are produced than usual.

Phalaenopsis 'Cool Breeze'
There are many varieties available today that make ideal houseplants and the white hybrids are no exception. Originally bred from the species *P. amabilis*, they have proved to be very tolerant and free flowering. The large blooms can last for many weeks in perfect condition when kept in a warm, light position. To encourage frequent reflowering when the first set of flowers has died, cut the stem back to the next eye and this will soon branch and produce more buds.

Phalaenopsis venosa x *violacea*
Two miniature phalaenopsis have been crossed together to produce a very brightly colored novelty hybrid. The flowers stay low to the foliage and, although only produced in small numbers at a time, flower for a long time with buds being produced in succession. One of the parents, *P. violacea*, is fragrant and this tends to come out in its hybrids making them more desirable. Fairly large, rounded leaves are also a characteristic of these *Phalaenopsis* types.

PLEIONE

Pleione is a comparatively small genus, with species growing mostly in northern India and China. They are to be found on both sides of the Himalayan range. Here they grow either as terrestrial plants in the ground, as lithophytes on cliff faces or rocks, or on trees as epiphytes. In fact, they can be found almost anywhere that their roots can grow in a good covering of moss. The habit of growth is very distinct and quite different from other orchids. The plant makes a pseudobulb each season and the previous year's pseudobulb will die back immediately, unlike other orchids which keep their old pseudobulbs for many years, forming large clusters. When the season's growth is complete, the plant will have produced a conical pseudobulb with a single leaf from the apex.

At the end of the growing season, these leaves turn yellow and drop off. The plant now enters a prolonged rest, which coincides in nature with the dry season. At the end of the rest a new shoot will appear at the base of the pseudobulb and quickly produce a large flower bud, or sometimes two. Shortly after the flower (or flowers) has faded, the base of this shoot continues to grow and forms the new pseudobulb. Upon its completion, the old pseudobulb will have withered away. A single *Pleione* plant never consists of more than one pseudobulb at a time. However, it is capable of producing two or three shoots from the base, which rapidly increases the stock. Also, the previous year's pseudobulb is capable of producing a mass of small bulblets from its apex, which again enables the plant to propagate quickly.

Cultivation of Pleiones

In cultivation, the growing season coincides with our summers and the plants rest throughout the winter. The exceptions are *Pleione maculata* and *P. praecox*, which produce their new shoots and flowers in the autumn. They grow slowly through the winter, finally completing their growth in late spring before going into a short summer rest.

Nearly all the species and hybrids require cool conditions and suit alpine houses that maintain a minimum winter nighttime temperature of just above freezing. Overwintering pleiones in these conditions, particularly the species *P. formosana*, results in good flowering in the forthcoming spring. Keep completely dry at this time of the year and no harm will come to the pseudobulbs.

Repotting is normally carried out annually at the first sign of new shoots. These quickly make new root systems and grow rapidly throughout the summer. Never allow the soil to become dry during this period; water even daily in hot, summer weather and fertilize regularly at the same time.

There are a variety of soils that seem to suit them. With their fine, hair-like roots, a mixture of fine bark and perlite with chopped sphagnum moss or sphagnum peat is ideal. The soil should not be firm, but loose; press the pseudobulb gently into it. Greater impact is achieved by growing up to 20 pseudobulbs in a single shallow pan filled with soil. This method of culture produces a stunning display of flowers. If the pseudobulbs are potted just before flowering, the shoots can be arranged so they all face the same direction, resulting in an even display of blooms.

The flowers are very large compared to the size of the pseudobulb. They range from white (*P. formosana* var. *alba*), through mauves and pale lilacs (the varieties of *P. formosana*) to the pure yellows, which are more difficult to grow.

In recent years there has been an increase in the interest in this small but fascinating group of plants. Much hybridizing has been carried out, producing new and improved strains with larger and more colorful flowers.

Left: *Pleione formosana.*

Pleione formosana

This is perhaps the best known of these dainty little orchids. It is the most easily cultivated and propagated and is thus often chosen by first-time orchid growers. Its rounded pseudobulbs are tinged with purple, reflecting the lavender-purple of the flowers. The lip is mainly white with reddish-brown spotting, making it a very pretty little flower. Several new shoots can be produced at a time so these plants multiply easily over the years into a large group of flowers every spring.

Pleione formosana var. alba

This is the only pure white albino *Pleione* in wide cultivation and, with only a touch of yellow in the throat, is an ideal companion to the pink species. When not in flower, the difference is seen in the pure apple-green pseudobulbs. The plants tend to be less strong and have smaller flowers than the species but this is typical of albino varieties. Other variations of *P. formosana* can also be found with white flowers and a red spotted lip, and various shades of pink flowers.

Pleione maculata

There are many species of *Pleione*, and many have pink-purple flowers in spring. This one does not. It is one of only two species that bloom in autumn. They complete their summer growth earlier and produce flowers in autumn just as their new growths start to move slowly through the winter. They tend to start growing as early as December. The flowers are large and white with deep red splashes over the hairy lip. Their culture is the same as the spring flowerers, only the watering regime should be adjusted according to when they begin to grow.

Pleione 'Piton'

Most pleiones have their flowers on relatively short stems, so the blooms are just above the developing foliage not far above the soil. This hybrid has a tall flower stem holding the bloom at around 4 in. (10 cm) high. The blooms are larger, too, about 2 in. (6 cm) across and are a beautiful soft lilac with dark purple speckling on a pale lip. This *Pleione* really stands out.

Pleione 'Shantung'

A few different pleiones have a creamy-yellow coloring. *P.* 'Shantung' is perhaps the best-known hybrid in this range; there are many named clones, some of which have been awarded. The petals and sepals are creamy-yellow with varying degrees of peach blushing; the lip is mainly white with red spotting all over. This is a free-flowering variety which is still grown widely and is always available.

Pleione 'Versailles'

There have been many hybrids between the various pink *Pleione* species and this is a particularly rich-colored one with a very deeply-colored patterned lip. It is easy to grow and reproduces itself well over the years. None of the pleione flowers last very long, but will live longer if kept in very cool conditions. To extend the flowering season, keep some of the plants back in a cooler place to slow down their rate of growth.

Top: *Pleione formosana* var. *alba*.

Above: *Pleione* 'Shantung Ridgeway' AM/RHS.

Left: *Pleione* 'Versailles'.

Below left: *Pleione* 'Piton'.

Below right: *Pleione maculata*.

VANDA ALLIANCE

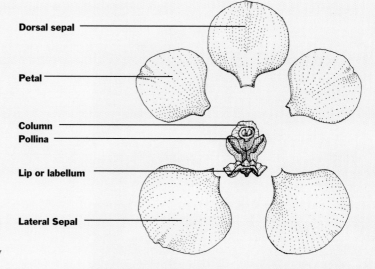

Dorsal sepal

Petal

Column
Pollina

Lip or labellum

Lateral Sepal

The genus *Vanda* consists of orchids that are found throughout tropical Southeast Asia. They are monopodial plants consisting of a single upright stem from which leaves are produced alternately, resulting in the plant appearing to be flat with new foliage constantly being produced from the top of the stem. The thick leaves can vary from soft and fleshy to very hard, depending on the particular species. The flower stem comes from the side, usually from the axil between the leaves. The roots are developed at the base of the plant, spreading in all directions. These plants are epiphytic in nature and ramble through their host tree.

There are many closely related orchids, including the ever-popular *Phalaenopsis*. It is possible to hybridize between *Vanda* and *Phalaenopsis*; the resulting offspring are called *Vandanopsis*. While some of these crosses can be very attractive, there has been little work done with this type of hybridizing. Vandas are more often crossed with some of their more closely related genera such as *Aerides*, *Rhynchostylis*, and *Ascocenda*, producing a huge range of complex hybrids in many colors, shapes, and sizes. These plants are more at home in tropical areas such as the West Indies, Florida, Thailand, the Malay Peninsula, and Singapore. Here they are grown extensively as garden plants, either in shade houses or established on large trees. Under these conditions they thrive and are almost continuously flowering. Some of the varieties grow and flower in such profusion and with such ease that they are grown extensively for cut flowers. Large quantities are shipped all over the world to meet the demand for inexpensive cut flower orchids.

In their native habitat, most *Vanda* species grow as epiphytes, high in the branches of the rainforest, where in the dry season they are subjected to long periods of drought. They retain moisture in their thick leaves and extensive root systems.

Above: The *Vanda* flower dissected to show various flower parts.

Care and Cultivation
In cultivation, these plants like to be grown in small wooden baskets hung on wires, with some protection from strong sunlight. Their long, aerial roots hang suspended from the base of the basket and can be sprayed and fertilized daily. Large nurseries with house after house of blooming vandas are a sight to behold. In cooler climates, they can be successfully grown as greenhouse plants. Hang them in the same way, without soil in wooden baskets, just relying on water and fertilizer sprayed on the roots. These orchids are the nearest we see to true air plants, deriving all their nourishment in this way. Unlike their cousins, the *Phalaenopsis*, they do not make good houseplants. While the *Phalaenopsis* will thrive in the warm, dry atmosphere of a centrally heated room, vandas require far more

humidity and light. To be really successful in cool climates they must be grown in a greenhouse.

Hybrids
The most popular plants are those that have *Vanda coerulea* in their background. This high-altitude, cool-growing species from the Himalayas grows on evergreen oaks and is sometimes subjected to near-freezing conditions. It is highly treasured for its pale blue forms with the darkest coming from northern Thailand and Burma. This is now difficult to obtain. Highly protected in their wild state, the only available plants are those raised in nurseries. When crossed with the lowland vandas, such as *Vanda sanderiana*, the result is a rich tessellated blue flower called *Vanda* 'Rothschildiana' which is tolerant of both high and low temperatures and is

the most popular variety grown in cooler parts of the world. It can be found in many shades of patterned blue, will last many months in bloom and will often flower twice a year.

Distant Relations

Across the Indian Ocean, in Africa, there are distant relatives, collectively known as the angraecums. This African family has the same habit of growth and resembles the vandas in every way except the flowers, which are strikingly different. They are large and white with long spurs at the back of the flower. This genus is seldom hybridized with the vandas or any of their close relatives. If any breeding has been done at all it is between the different species of *Angraecum* or other closely related African monopodials. Some of the most striking of these plants are to be found in Madagascar, where they have been isolated from the mainland of Africa for thousands of years and have evolved into very amazing plants.

Right:
Ascocenda 'Thai Joy'.

Below:
Ascocenda Crownfox 'Sunshine'.

Ascocenda 'Thai Joy'

There is now a very wide range of extremely vibrant colors in the *Vanda* Alliance and this is partly due to the introduction of the related genera *Ascocentrum* into the breeding. When crossed with a *Vanda*, the result is usually smaller flowers but a lot more of them and much brighter colors in pinks, yellows, and oranges. They need the same degree of warmth, light and high humidity to thrive and then they will often produce flowers twice a year.

Ascocenda 'Crownfox Sunshine'

The incredibly subtle and beautiful pale lemon yellow of this hybrid is something that is now being seen more often as a whole new palette of colors is emerging in the *Vanda* Alliance hybrids. Good light is the key to making them flower, so the best position is to hang them from the roof of the greenhouse.

Vanda coerulea

Blue is a color rarely seen in orchids and although this orchid is commonly described as blue it is probably more lilac in reality. However, this orchid has been instrumental in the breeding of "blue" vandas, which have become the most popular of all the modern *Vanda* hybrids. *V. coerulea* is a cool-growing species from the Himalayan mountains. This is why its offspring have been so widely grown as they tend to inherit this cool temperature tolerance. The species itself is not that widely available as it is slow to grow in cultivation, but the hybrids are often seen and with a cool, light, and humid environment can be grown with relative success.

Vanda cristata

Whereas many of the modern *Vanda* hybrids are large and highly colorful, many of the species are a little more subdued and dainty. This is not to say they do not have an appeal which is seen in this charming species from the high mountains of the Himalayas in India and Nepal. *Vanda cristata* is a cool-growing species that is more easily accommodated in the cooler parts of the world and, because of its small stature and pretty flowers, is an ideal plant for the amateur's mixed collection. Several stems of one or two small green flowers can be produced at one time in the spring. The cream lip, with its almost black center, shows the flowers up to good effect.

Above: *Vanda cristata.*

Below left: *Vanda coerulea.*

Below right: *Vanda suavis* var. *tricolor.*

Far right: *Vanda 'Rothschildiana'.*

Vanda suavis var. tricolor

This species from Java is one of the most flamboyant of the vandas. This warm-growing orchid produces a tall flower spike with many large and showy blooms. The curled-back petals and sepals have a white or cream background and are brightly spotted and patterned in reddish brown. The lip forms the third color of purple hence its varietal name. Mature plants of this species can flower twice a year and last for many weeks each time. It is certainly one of the more unusual of the *Vanda* species and is well worth trying if you have a humid, warm orchid house in which to grow it.

Vanda 'Rothschildiana'

Probably the most famous of all the *Vanda* hybrids, this is a primary hybrid between the species *V. coerulea* and *V. sanderiana*. The first species gives the plant a tolerance of cooler temperatures and a marvelous shade of blue, while the second increases the size of the flower and gives it the characteristic tessellation over the bloom. *V. sanderiana* is also warmer-growing so, *V.* 'Rothschildiana' is in fact happy in either a warm or a cool position. Experience has found, though, that these orchids often bloom more easily and frequently if kept at a minimum of 50° F (10° C) rather than a warmer temperature.

UNUSUAL ORCHIDS

If you have a few orchids already and wish to add to your collection, the following plants make interesting subjects. Many are favored by collectors who like something unusual and sometimes they are rather challenging to grow, but the extra effort will be well repaid. Many make ideal companion plants for each other, or excellent additions to mixed collections.

BIFRENARIA

These plants originate mostly in Brazil. *Bifrenaria* is a small genus without great diversity. The plants grow mainly as epiphytes, but will grow as terrestrials where the drainage suits them best. Each plant consists of a series of hard, dark green, conical pseudobulbs. From the top of each pseudobulb arises a single, large, plicate, very hard leaf. This stout foliage grows upright from the pseudobulb and is kept for several years before being discarded. Flower spikes, as with most orchids, come from the base of the leading pseudobulb. They can produce one or two blooms which are large and very attractive. The petals and sepals are of a uniform size with rounded tips. Their color can vary depending on the species, from greeny-white through to deep rosy-pink and the small, broad lip is usually dark mauve or red. All species have a fragrance.

The most popular species is *Bifrenaria harrisoniae*. This has a pleasing perfume and the plants will grow into large clumps in hanging baskets or pots. Other species such as *B. tyrianthina* have darker petals and a less intense perfume. There are a few hybrids in the genus but little breeding has been carried out.

Caring for Bifrenarias

If grown in a warm area of the greenhouse, most bifrenarias have a distinct resting and growing period. As is often the case with orchids that are expected to grow in the summer and rest in the winter, there is always the odd plant that will do the opposite. While the plant is producing active growth and roots, it should be kept freely watered and fertilized. When there appears to be no activity, keep it on the dry side to avoid any infection or rotting of the roots. As is typical of this type of orchid, the new growth and flower spikes are liable to emerge at the same time, a good indication that watering should recommence.

BRASSIA

The genus *Brassia* is closely related to *Odontoglossum* and *Oncidium* and, although it will happily hybridize with these plants, it is a genus that stands out on its own. Therefore it is best to consider it separately from its relatives.

Brassia are distributed throughout South America, on numerous West Indian islands, and as far north as Mexico. They are usually found growing on trees in large clumps. The dark green, plum-shaped pseudobulbs have two terminal leaves and are separated by a short rhizome. The flower spikes usually appear shortly after the completion of the season's growth and will grow slowly for several months before producing buds. Depending on the species, these spikes are 20–40 in. (50–100cm) in length. Each spike will carry ten or twelve very large flowers. Each bloom consists of ribbon-like petals which stick out firmly from the center of the flower. This gives the appearance of a starburst or spider, hence the common name of spider orchid. Most of these flowers are pale green or yellow, some bordering on orange; some speckling may occur in the center of the bloom. The lip, shorter and broader than the petals, is similarly marked. Many of the flowers within this genus have a strong perfume, which adds to their attraction. However, the scent is lost in hybridization.

Although a number of the species will grow best in cool conditions, many are tolerant of higher temperatures, adding to their usefulness when breeding.

The main species is *B. verrucosa* from Mexico and Guatemala, one of the most common with its pale green flowers on long spikes. It is easily grown by the amateur and will flower freely under most conditions. It does prefer more light than some of the other related genera. Popular hybrids include *B.* 'Rex', which has large colorful blooms that are likely to be produced in any season of the year. Many hybrids have appeared when the plant has been bred with other genera, including oncidiums, odontoglossums and miltonias. There are numerous other hybrids resulting from crossing three genera together, the most famous being *Maclellaneara* and *Beallara*.

BULBOPHYLLUM & CIRRHOPETALUM

Some authorities put these two genera together and call them both *Bulbophyllum*, while others are busy subdividing them into smaller groups. However they are classified, they represent a very large number of plants, which are widely distributed throughout the tropical world, with members of the family on all continents.

They are bulbous orchids usually producing rounded, dark green pseudobulbs with a single large leaf at the top. The flower spikes are produced from the base of the plant and, due to the large number of different species, the flower shapes differ considerably. Many are very small and are only of botanical interest while others have large, curiously interesting flowers. These differences make them attractive to the specialist grower.

In the wild and in cultivation they will grow into large clumps. With little attention they will thrive, lasting for many years and giving an annual display of blooms without the need of disturbance.

Some species, such as *Cirrhopetalum umbellatum*, will give a large head of pale pink flowers while others, such as *C. guttulatum*, produce dainty, pale green flowers with a peppered ring of spots. The *Bulbophyllum* group come from Africa and produce tall flower spikes that are broad, flattened, and sometimes twisted. The flowers are small and insignificant, appearing like insects crawling up the spike. The most noted species is *B. purpureorachis*, also known as the Zulu spear orchid.

Some of the largest plants in the genus come from New Guinea. *B. fletcherianum*, for example, has enormous pseudobulbs, as big as goose eggs, and huge leaves up to 3 ft. (1 m) long. It is so heavy that the plant hangs down from its host tree. From the base of the plant comes an array of large purple and red fleshy blooms, blessed with an horrific odor attracting the carrion flies or wasps that pollinate them. Other bulbophyllums from this part of the world, such as *B. graveolans* with golden yellow flowers, also produce a very strong and unpleasant smell. These plants are often found in botanical gardens as curiosities, rather than in private collections.

A fascinating feature of this group of orchids is that the lip moves quite freely with the slightest

Above:
Bulbophyllum watsonianum enjoys growing around the outside of its wooden basket.

breeze or touch. *B. lobbii* has a lip that will rotate back underneath the flower and then spring back into its original position. *B. barbigerum* has small flowers resembling a flying insect such as a gnat or mosquito. A slight movement will send the whole spike waving. The lip consists of a mass of very fine hairs enabling it to move on the breeze. *B. medusae* produces numerous flowers at the end of a long stem, formed in a cluster. The thin, cotton-like petals hang down, giving it its name.

Considering the size of the genus, very little hybridizing has been done but there is the scope to produce strange and unusual flowers. The most famous of the all the hybrids is *Cirrhopetalum* 'Elizabeth Ann' with its long, pale pink, patterned petals making it a most attractive orchid to grow.

CALANTHE

Calanthes are distributed throughout southern China, across Japan, most of India, down through Thailand, the Malay Peninsula, and various islands of Southeast Asia. They are terrestrials, growing in various types of soil or on rocky outcrops, thriving wherever the conditions suit them best.

This genus can be roughly divided into two groups, the evergreen and the deciduous plants. Firstly, the evergreen calanthes produce a creeping rhizome either just on or just below the surface of the soil. Along the rhizome grow two, three, or four leaves from a very small pseudobulb. The new growth appears at the end of the rhizome and quickly matures into fresh foliage, usually flowering at the same time. The flower spikes stand upright, well clear of the leaves, which is typical of any terrestrial orchid. The sprays of flowers come in a range of colors, from browny-yellows to bright gold, through to white.

The very first orchid hybrid was created from two evergreen *Calanthe* species. It was produced in 1856, between *C. masuca* and *C. furcata* and was named *Calanthe* 'Dominii'.

The Victorians grew large quantities of beautiful calanthes. Cool-growing and requiring little or no artificial heat, large pans of these plants would decorate their huge conservatories. Sadly, today they are out of fashion and few people grow them. The exception being in the Far East, particularly Japan, where they have always been popular and remain so today. A visitor to a Japanese orchid show will see large displays of modern hybrids, all beautifully grown.

The deciduous calanthes come from a similar part of the world but are not as widely distributed. Their vegetative parts are very different, producing large, stout pseudobulbs, silvery white in color. They carry two or three enormous terminal leaves which are extremely thin as they are not designed to last for long.

The season starts in the spring with the new growth; at this point the plants should be repotted. Give copious amounts of water and fertilizer throughout the summer and you will find that nothing grows as fast as a *Calanthe*. The pseudobulbs become fully grown in record time and on completion the flower spike, or spikes, will appear from the base. At this time the leaves deteriorate rapidly and will soon be shed. When this happens, reduce the watering and then eventually stop altogether. The older pseudobulb from which the new growth came will deteriorate but can sometimes be used for propagation. The flower spikes will continue to grow all through the autumn and winter, relying on the energy stored in the pseudobulb.

The flower stems can reach 3 ft. (1 m) in height with blooms ranging from white, cream with red lips, through various shades of pink to the deepest reds. Once in flower they are extremely long-lasting, remaining in perfect condition for many months. This was why they were popular with the Victorians who brought them indoors for displaying, without the need to water. As the plants have lost their leaves and most of their roots by then, watering is not necessary. As soon as the flowers have finished the spikes are removed and the spring growth is ready to begin.

One hundred years ago, when calanthes were at their most popular, there were many varieties. Hybridization had increased and the selection was large. These orchids went out of fashion as happens with many plants, but a few plants lingered on in private collections until the 1980s when a renewed interest led to further hybridizing. The result is that today we have a larger range of shapes and sizes than ever before, and those with the necessary space will find them most rewarding to grow.

COELOGYNE

This is a large genus of mainly epiphytic orchids from tropical Asia, found as far north as China, throughout the whole of India, Sri Lanka, Burma, the Malay Peninsula, and as far south as New Guinea.

Most of them have large, attractive flowers and even out of bloom they are very interesting plants. They have fat green pseudobulbs, each with two terminal leaves, joined together with a hard woody creeping rhizome. They are at home in the fork or on the branches of large trees where they will keep their old pseudobulbs and foliage for many years. Many species have the habit of flowering from the center of the potential new growth and most flower in spring in cultivation. New shoots start to appear in late winter and quickly develop. After flowering, the shoots continue to grow and become the new pseudobulbs, completing their growth by the autumn. The plants then have a short or long rest, depending on the species, for the duration of the winter.

While they are growing, the plants enjoy great amounts of water and fertilizer to ensure that the new shoots produce fat, healthy pseudobulbs in late summer. It was once thought that these orchids should be kept bone dry all winter but this will lead to excessive shriveling and it will take a lot of effort to improve them by the following growing season. By staying just moist throughout the winter, they can maintain plump pseudobulbs all the year round.

Plants from the Himalayas are dominated by such species as *C. cristata, C. ochracea, C. corymbosa,* and *C. flaccida.* All of these species produce beautiful, shimmering white flowers with bright golden or orange lip patterns. The enormous clumps stand out in their natural habitats. In cultivation, such orchids flowering in the late winter and spring can fill the greenhouse with their perfume.

Hailing from areas further south, species such as *C. massangeana* and *C. dayana* produce long pendent flower spikes which makes them unsuitable for bench culture.

They are best grown hanging up in baskets or pots suspended from the roof of the greenhouse. These long flower spikes, up to 24 in. (60 cm), consist of dozens of creamy white flowers with brown centers and this coloring makes them very attractive.

One of the most sought-after species is *C. pandurata* with its pale apple-green petals and very dark, almost black, lip. This earns it the common name of black orchid.

Below:
Coelogyne fuliginosa.

There are few hybrid coelogynes, mainly because they prove very difficult to breed. But those hybrids that do exist are famous. *Coelogyne* 'Green Dragon Burnham', a hybrid from *C. pandurata* and *C. massangeana,* has very long pendent spikes with the best qualities of both parents. *Coelogyne* 'Memoria William Micholitz', with its glistening white blooms, is a hybrid between *C. mooreana* and *C. lawrenceana.*

There seem to be very few close relatives of the coelogynes and therefore it is not surprising that there are hybrids with other genera. Although the color range is limited, mostly whites, browns, yellows, and greens, the prospect for hybridizing should be tempting. The chance to create new shapes and improve the varieties seems well worthwhile.

ENCYCLIA

Encyclias are widely distributed throughout tropical America, both north and south, and the islands of the West Indies. They are bulbous orchids producing either long and slender or short and fat pseudobulbs, with terminal foliage consisting of two, three, or even four leaves. Flower spikes are always produced from the top of the pseudobulb, generally from the previous season's growth. The blooms are held on upright spikes and come in a fascinating range of colors. The plants are usually epiphytes and, depending on the species, can be small, scrubby bushes or large specimen plants found only on large trees. They can also be found growing on the ground or on rocky outcrops where the environment is suitable.

This is a large genus which, over the years, has been divided and reclassified several times, originally being part of the genus *Epidendrum*. Recently it has had more taxonomic changes with many of the species being placed in the genus *Prosthechea*. However, they are still widely known as encyclias. They have been bred for many years and for the purpose of hybridization, they are recorded as epidendrums when making crosses between genera. Hybrids within the genus itself are few and far between but when crossed with other related plants, such as the cattleyas, they produce some wonderfully colorful hybrids and small, compact plants.

One of the best known of the encyclias is *E. cochleata* which was one of the earliest orchids introduced into cultivation in the West, as long ago as 1763.

Most of the species require cool conditions, although some will flourish just as well in the intermediate or hot house. As they are widely distributed, they are equally diverse in their cultural requirements. The cool varieties do not have strict growing and resting seasons as do some of our other orchids. The best rule is to follow the plant and if it decides to grow throughout the winter then it should be watered even if the one beside it prefers to rest with less water until the new roots and growth commence.

EPIDENDRUM

These orchids are found throughout tropical America and the West Indies, where they grow either as epiphytes or as terrestrials. Most of the epidendrums have long, thin, cane-like stems, the length of which can vary from 2 in. (5 cm) to 10 ft. (3 m). The flowers are produced from the top of the stem and some species are almost continuously blooming, a succession of fresh flowers being produced for up to two or three years without rest.

The range of colors is extensive, from pale lettuce green to dark red, bright oranges, and yellows. These qualities make them very popular garden plants anywhere in the tropics and in many countries they are found growing wild, having escaped from their original gardens. In cooler climates they are ideal plants for the greenhouse or home.

Left:
Encyclia cochleata, also known as the Cockleshell Orchid.

Above:
Epidendrum radicans, also known as the Crucifix Orchid because of its cross-shaped lip.

Right:
Epidendrum ciliare.

The name *Epidendrum* is a very old one and was originally given to all orchids found growing on trees. Consequently, whenever new species were discovered they were automatically called *Epidendrum* with the result that many of the orchids that we grow today were formerly called *Epidendrum*. With improved classification, more and more plants have been taken out of this genus. The true epidendrums have been extensively hybridized resulting in larger more showy flowers for the tropical garden or temperate greenhouse. Reed-type epidendrums are remarkable plants, being tolerant and easily adapted to a variety of climates. They will thrive in any frost-free conditions and give the grower a rewarding show of flowers.

GONGORA

Gongoras come from mainland America. They all grow as epiphytes either in tropical or cool regions. Mostly they are high-altitude species growing in the cloud forests, on the trunks and branches of large trees. They produce a round to oval, ridged pseudobulb with two or three terminal leaves. The flower spikes all come from the base of the plant and are long, thin, and wiry with between four and fifteen blooms, or more in some species, which hang down in a pendent fashion. The blooms are curiously shaped and give the appearance of a flying insect, combined with a strong perfume. Their colors vary from yellow through tawny-brown to spotted red.

This is a genus that attracts the specialized grower who is looking for unusual orchids, but they do grow well in most amateur greenhouses. Due to their pendent habit, they are best accommodated in baskets or flower pots which are suspended from the roof of the greenhouse. Alternatively, they will do well on slabs of bark hung on the wall.

Their closest relatives are the stanhopeas but there are few records of them having been crossed with these orchids. However, there is room for breeding with the genus to produce novelty hybrids.

All the species are capable of growing into considerably large clumps which can be left as specimen plants or divided as the grower prefers.

Below:
Gongora galeata.

HUNTLEYA & PESCATOREA

These orchids are found on the mainland of South America, growing epiphytically and just occasionally terrestrially, in the cloud forests where the weather is almost permanently wet. Through evolution, these orchids have dispensed with pseudobulbs altogether and replaced them with large tufts of foliage. Five, six or more leaves in each tuft are separated by a short, thick, woody rhizome and as the new growth reaches maturity the flowers are produced at the same time.

As these orchids are lucky enough to grow in places where there is no prolonged dry period, they are able to keep their leaves all the year round and, thus, do not need food storage in the form of a pseudobulb. They are continuously growing and can flower at any time of the year. The blooms are borne singly from the base of the plant and often more than one will appear at a time.

There are numerous species, the most famous being *Huntleya meleagris*; its large, flat, star-shaped blooms with orange-brown petal tips and a paler center make this a stunning flower combined with a shiny, varnish-like finish. There are several other related genera that will do well given the same conditions. Examples of plants within these genera include *Pescatorea lawrenceana* with white, amethyst-tipped petals, *Bollea coelestes* with large, electric blue flowers, a color so seldom seen in orchids, and *Cochleanthes discolor* with a trumpet-shaped, purple lip and creamy pink petals.

All these orchids enjoy the high altitude of the mountains of South America, mainly in the Andes where they thrive in the moisture of the cloud forests for most of the year. It is, therefore, important never to let these plants get dry for too long and to keep them shaded from direct sun as their delicate foliage is easily scorched.

It seems a shame that such a beautiful group of orchids is not very popular and receives little attention. They are seldom hybridized, a missed opportunity with so many colors and shapes to choose from among the close relatives. Breeding from this stock would surely produce some very interesting blooms.

LUDISIA

Ludisia is a small genus of terrestrial, occasionally epiphytic, orchids mostly from Southeast Asia, commonly known as jewel orchids. This name can be generally applied to all the plants that have attractive foliage but, without doubt, *Ludisia* is the finest.

The plant consists of a short creeping rhizome along which the leaves are produced at intervals, terminating in a rosette of foliage. From its center comes the flower spike. Once that growth has flowered it produces a new shoot from the base and the process of growth is repeated. The leaves have a beautiful velvet-like appearance and feel, and are colored deep green or maroon with red or orange veining. The patterns on each of the species or even on each individual plant can vary considerably.

The flower spike, produced at the end of the season's growth, stands erect, clearing any surrounding foliage. The flowers are small and white with yellow centers, as seen in the most popular and most commonly cultivated species, *L. discolor*.

Grow in a mixture of fine bark, peat, or leafmold with some coarse grit or sand to keep the soil open. Pot loosely in shallow pots or pans to accommodate the creeping rhizome. Shade well from all direct sun, but maintain good light. This is a forest floor plant and therefore should not become completely dry. Do not spray the leaves with hard water or insecticides, as both of these will leave deposits and spoil the appearance of the foliage.

This orchid will grow well as a houseplant on a sideboard or window sill and can be admired all the year round. In the past, they were grown under bell jars for display and to increase the humidity around the plants. Many of the species formerly in cultivation are difficult to find today and only appear in specialized collections. There are numerous other closely related terrestrial orchids with these beautiful markings and they are well worth seeking out.

Above:
Ludisia discolor,
the Jewel
Orchid.

LYCASTE & ANGULOA

The genus *Lycaste* has always been popular with amateur growers. These plants are easy to grow, flower freely, and have large decorative blooms. They are found mainly in the Andes of South America, with numerous representatives as far north as Guatemala and tropical Mexico. The plants either grow as terrestrial orchids or as epiphytes depending on the particular species. They all produce round or oval pseudobulbs, closely joined together, and as a rule they have two large leaves at the apex. On a large plant, the leaves can appear somewhat untidy and are never kept on the plant for very long. This is annual foliage, which is discarded during the resting season. Some lycastes in cultivation may keep their leaves for another year but this is the exception rather than the rule. As with all deciduous orchids, the foliage is soft and not designed to last and this makes it vulnerable to spotting and general disfiguration as the leaf ages quickly. Growers may prefer to remove the leaves when they become too unsightly, to improve the appearance of their plant.

These orchids usually flower during their resting season and the best hybrids produce a profusion of blooms from around the base of the leading pseudobulb. Each flower is borne on a single stem and it is possible to have 20 or so blooms from one pseudobulb. In many cases these large, attractive flowers are highly scented. During the flowering season it is best to keep the plants on the dry side, which enables the blooms to last longer, and prevents spotting.

The new growth will quickly appear when flowering has finished, or sometimes even at the same time. In the short but fast growing season, give plenty of water and fertilizer to encourage as large a pseudobulb as possible before the season's growth is completed. When resting begins, give less water, although there are no hard and fast rules as they will not all grow in the summer and all rest in the winter. Just remember that if it is growing, water it; if it is resting, don't.

The soft, tender leaves make this orchid susceptible to aphid attack. It does not like to be sprayed with any form of insecticide, as foliage burn will result, so using water and a sponge is the best way to control this pest.

Most famous of all the species is *L. skinnerii*, sometimes known as *L. virginalis*, a species from Guatemala with huge pink flowers. It is seldom seen in cultivation today but at one time was so popular that collections would be made of all the different color forms, from pure white and soft pink to the darkest of rose-colored blooms. Other species include *L. aromatica* and *L. cruenta*, with their golden yellow sepals and greenish petals. The greenhouse will be filled with their perfume.

Some terrestrial species arise in South America and these have to grow in competition with many other plants on the ground. Because of this, they have developed long foliage and equally long flower stems. One of these is *L. locusta* which has dark green flowers.

Closely related to *Lycaste* is the genus *Anguloa*. These plants are mostly restricted to the higher altitudes of the Andes, Ecuador, Colombia, and Peru. Their vegetative parts and habit of growth are the same as the lycastes but they are somewhat more robust. They make larger plants and their big foliage at the height of the growing season makes them very demanding on the greenhouse space available.

Their cup-shaped flowers are borne on single stems, but never open fully, unlike the lycastes. This characteristic has earned them the name of tulip orchid.

The best known of them is *A. clowesii* with its brilliant yellow, strongly scented flowers. There are numerous other species with white and pink flowers, but the genus is not as large as the lycastes.

These two genera have been extensively hybridized since the earliest times, producing both hybrids within their own genera and intergeneric hybrids where members of the two different groups have been crossed together. The results are some outstandingly beautiful orchids, which are greatly sought after. These orchids make excellent houseplants, thriving well on a window sill in a cool room while resting, and being given warmth and light during the growing season. Their delicate foliage should be protected from direct sunlight through glass, to prevent scorching.

MASDEVALLIA

Masdevallia is one of those huge genera that contains so many species with such a diversity of flowers that it is almost impossible to generalize. They are all native to the Americas, the majority found at high altitudes either in the coastal range of mountains in Brazil or in the Andes, where they are found in great profusion, and as far north as the rainforests of Mexico.

They are generally small, tufted plants without pseudobulbs and each season's growth consists of a single leaf. Many growths are produced at a time and the result is a large tuft of pale or dark green leaves. Without a pseudobulb to sustain the plant during periods of drought, the leaves have become very thick and can store moisture in great quantities. This conserves the orchid for short periods without rain. In nature, these plants are often found on moss-covered tree branches where their fine root system can grip and find enough moisture and nourishment to sustain the plant. They will be equally at home on mossy rocks or even on the ground where the drainage suits them and the competition from other plants is not too great.

The flowers are borne on a single stem and can be solitary or numerous. The sepals are the largest and most dominant part of the bloom with the petals and labellum so diminutive that they are hardly noticeable. The edges of the sepals are often fused, giving the appearance of a triangular or kite-shaped flower. The colors are as variable as the colors in a rainbow from pure whites, yellows, and browns, spotted and patterned, to some which are brilliant oranges, purples, and mauves.

There are many hundreds of species, most requiring no more than a small flower pot about the size of a coffee cup; a great many plants can be accommodated in a small greenhouse. Their size makes them eagerly sought after by specialized growers and there are many collectors who grow only this one attractive genus. As they are high-altitude plants their temperature requirements are not great; they enjoy cool, moist conditions all year. It is as important to ensure that they do not overheat on a hot summer's day as to make sure that they don't get too cold on a severe winter's night. In the wild, they are not subjected to long droughts so do not need resting periods.

It takes a sharp eye and a steady hand to pollinate these flowers but considerable hybridizing has been done within this group and there is plenty of scope for more. With many species to choose from, combined with their readiness to breed, the chances for hybridizing are great. Once the seedlings are established they grow quickly and will bloom in a short time from sowing: two to three years compared with twice that for many other orchids.

A large group of other genera are related to the masdevallias, including the draculas whose flowers are huge compared to the plant. Large, triangular blooms with long, thin, pointed tips are produced in sequence from the same stem and although short-lived, they have a curious attraction with their lip structure. The flowers are highly patterned and have a mysterious quality about them that makes them live up to their name.

Dryadella, a genus of small compact orchids, is also closely related and has stemless flowers nestling around the base of the plant, giving it the common name of pheasant in the grass.

An even larger group than *Masdevallia* is *Pleurothallis*. Most of these plants have very small, insignificant blooms but are still worth growing by the amateur who likes to possess something different. These genera grow well together in a cool, well-shaded greenhouse.

Below: *Masdevallia coccinea.*

MILTONIA

This genus has suffered drastically from reclassification and many plants that were formerly listed under this heading have been removed to other genera. Thus the true miltonias are a smaller group than they used to be, but many of them that have been reclassified are still commonly classed as miltonias, particularly for breeding and hybridization purposes.

The true miltonias are found mostly in Brazil where they produce somewhat flattened, elongated pseudobulbs separated from each other on a creeping rhizome. They are good climbers and make themselves at home on most tree species. Here they will quickly cover a tree trunk, their long rhizomes dividing into many branches. Their foliage is pale green, which is an indication that the plant prefers shade. However, in cultivation, good light does seem to be an important factor in their requirements.

Flower spikes are produced with the onset of the new growth, bearing two or three flowers. The large, broad lip dominates these blooms. The petals are of equal size, but slightly narrower.

The most famous of all the species is *Miltonia spectabilis*, with its pale pink petals and richly veined darker pink lip. In the variety *moreliana*, the petals are an extremely dark, rosy pink with an even darker patterned lip. Other species such as *M. flavescens* produce long spikes of eight to ten flowers, in pale straw yellow.

Most of them are found in the Brazilian rainforests, growing at various altitudes depending on the species. In cultivation this orchid is not difficult to grow in the intermediate or warm greenhouse. It often develops a dislike of pot culture and quickly finds its way over the rim where it will make a copious amount of aerial roots. Such species do well in hanging baskets or mounted on slabs of cork bark or tree fern. They have little or no resting period so as fast as the new growths are completed, others are produced, usually two or three at a time. This results in a large, bushy plant which adds to its attraction and is well worth accommodating.

Miltonias, particularly *M. spectabilis*, have been used for hybridizing, not only within the genus but also with genera such as odontoglossums, producing intergeneric hybrids. These produce flowers resembling odontoglossums but they are heat tolerant and capable of being grown in warmer climates.

STANHOPEA

Stanhopeas are orchids that everybody admires. They are among the largest of the orchid blooms and are very strongly scented. They are all native to tropical America, found both north and south of the Panama Isthmus. They also occur on a number of the islands of the West Indies where they grow as epiphytes, making large clumps in the forks or on the main branches of mature trees. The plants consist of a dark green conical pseudobulb with a single, hard leaf produced from the apex. The most extraordinary feature is the flower spike, which grows from the base. Instead of growing outwards or upwards from the plant, it penetrates straight down and produces its flowers as a pendant spike from beneath the plant. This is perfect for a plant growing as an epiphyte where the spikes can easily grow through the root ball or moss at the base of the orchid and can flower freely. In cultivation, however, they are suitable only for growing in baskets suspended from the roof of the greenhouse. If they are grown in pots, the plant will thrive but the flower spike will never appear out of the pot.

In the case of most orchids, the flower spikes are slow to develop and the buds, as they open, may take several days or weeks to become perfect blooms. The stanhopeas are quite different. The spike grows rapidly and the buds are larger than any other orchid when fully mature. At this stage, they burst open producing a fully developed, complete bloom, within a few minutes. These enormous flowers, with their fantastic shape, color and patterning, will last barely a week in perfection, which is just long enough for them to become pollinated in the wild.

Even within one easily identifiable species of *Stanhopea*, the color patterning of the flower can vary considerably, as can the shape and size of the bloom. This means that it is difficult for one species to be distinguished from another and, apart from this tremendous variation within a single species, there is also much natural hybridization taking place. This produces populations of hybrids mixed in with the naturally occurring species, which makes a challenging situation for any taxonomist. As a result, the genus *Stanhopea* seems to be under constant revision.

The most commonly cultivated species are *S. tigrina*, with its deep maroon patterning on a pale cream flower, and *S. oculata*, which is yellow with finely peppered petals and a dark eye at the base of the lip.

Apart from the natural hybridization, there is much scope for anyone wishing to venture into the breeding of these orchids. They pollinate freely and give many seeds. It is disappointing that the blooms do not last longer. Every collection should have room for a few hanging baskets either in the cool or intermediate house, as the *Stanhopea* is an easily accommodated orchid.

Left: *Mintonia spectabilis* var. *moreliana*.

Below left: *Stanhopea oculata*.

THUNIA

This is a small group of orchids coming mostly from the Himalayas where they have very distinct resting and growing seasons. They can be found growing either on the ground or on rocks or trees. As terrestrial plants they have a short, very fast growing season. The new growth starts with the rainy season or, in cultivation, with the onset of spring. The small growths are easily damped off until they are 2–3 in. (5–8 cm) high, by which time they will have established a root system and be growing well. From then onwards, give plenty of water and fertilizer to ensure they reach maturity.

The plants produce long, cane-like pseudobulbs, measuring anything up to 3 ft. (1 m) in length with soft papery leaves produced alternately along the full length of the canes. Immediately when the pseudobulbs are mature they produce a large head of flowers from the top. In most cases, the petals are a pure brilliant white with large, frilly, flame-colored lips.

Once the plants have finished flowering, they will have stopped growing for the season and within a month or two the foliage starts to die, putting on a bright display of autumn colors, just before falling off. This leaves the stout, leafless, elongated pseudobulb bearing a close resemblance to the horn of an antelope. No water or fertilizer is needed until the plant starts to grow again in the spring. The previous season's pseudobulb will, by now, have completely shriveled up and died, passing all its energy on to the new one. A single plant never consists of more than one pseudobulb at a time. During the growing season, it is important to keep the plant heavily shaded, to protect its delicate pale green foliage from scorching.

The most notable species is *Thunia marshalliana*, which produces the largest and most colorful lip of all the species. There are several hybrids; the best of these is *Thunia* 'Gattonense' which has pale pink petals and a dark rosy pink lip with yellow markings. There is little scope for hybridizing within this genus as it does not seem to have any close relatives and the color range is limited. They make good companions for plants such as the deciduous calanthes whose culture and requirements are very similar.

ZYGOPETALUM

These plants are found throughout tropical South America, mostly in the higher mountain regions of the Andes and the Atlantic coastal range. It is a small but very attractive group of species which usually grow as terrestrials or occasionally as epiphytes, with one species growing as a climber. These are evergreen orchids, which produce a series of pseudobulbs along a creeping rhizome with basal and terminal foliage. The flower spike is produced at the same time as the new growth. The dominating feature of the blooms is the large and very colorful lip. The base color is white or cream with heavy striping and patterning in deep lilac. In some species the color is completely solid. The petals are a mixture of green and brown patterning and are nearly always strongly scented.

Although they originate near the Equator, most of these plants are from high altitudes and will do well in the cool greenhouse where they prefer a shady position.

The most popular of the species is *Z. intermedium*, which is commonly sold as *Z. mackayii*. It is the most robust growing of the species and produces long spikes of attractive flowers. *Z. crinitum* is a smaller, compact plant that is very highly scented. *Z. maxillare* has a long, thin rhizome and is best treated as a climber, trained up a fir pole with its base growing in a pot. The lip is an intense electric blue, making a wonderful contrast to the others with their violet lips.

Between these species there has been considerable hybridization resulting in the color being strengthened. They have also been crossed with closely related genera such as *Colax* and *Promenaea*.

ALPINE HOUSE ORCHIDS

So far we have been mainly looking at the tropical orchids, most of which grow as epiphytes on trees or occasionally on the ground when they have fallen from their host. There are, however, a large group of terrestrial plants that only grow in the soil. They can be found all over the world and in fact are more widely distributed than the epiphytes, which are limited to the rainforest regions. Terrestrial orchids can be found in the harshest of conditions, way up in the Arctic Circle or in dry dusty deserts or in open savannah and prairie country where no trees exist at all.

These plants can be grown in the garden or in an alpine greenhouse that is kept just frost-free. They offer the grower a wider choice of orchids, all as fascinating to cultivate as their epiphytic, tropical cousins. Some of these terrestrials will require a heated greenhouse with a minimum nighttime temperature of 40–50° F (5–10° C). Others will require just the simple protection of an unheated, alpine house, while the most hardy can be grown outside in a herbaceous border, where the drainage and soil suits them well and where they will flower freely.

Most terrestrial orchids start growing during the winter, slowly developing their new leaves and rapidly increasing their growth as the spring advances, culminating in a display of flowers. They then rest for the summer until they recommence growth when the cycle of the seasons is completed. Growing as an underground, creeping rhizome, quite deep where the soil permits, they produce a shoot each season, appearing above the ground as a rosette of leaves with the flower spike produced from the center.

Some of these orchids start to grow in the autumn and progress slowly all winter. Those species that grow wild in southern and eastern Mediterranean climates flower much earlier, with the result that they have completely died down below ground level by the time the hot, dry summer starts.

The high-altitude species growing in mountainous regions or the Arctic Circle cannot become active until the snows have receded. They then have a short, fast growing season culminating in flowers which must produce seeds before the winter returns.

At one time these terrestrial orchids were difficult to obtain. Specialized orchid nurseries that only grow alpine plants or hardy orchids are the best suppliers. When finding these plants growing wild in the country-side, it is tempting to remove them. However, as well as this practice being illegal in most countries, flowering time would be the wrong season to disturb them and this is when they are most visible. Specialized nurseries grow and propagate these plants from seed and can now offer a wide range of pot-grown stock.

Suitable Plants

Disa is a genus that comes from Africa. The most popular of these species, *Disa uniflora*, comes from Table Mountain in South Africa and has a range of hybrids which produce the most brilliant bright reds, oranges, and yellows. These orchids are best grown in a specialized greenhouse with a winter nighttime temperature of 45–50° F (8–10° C) with bright sunny days and large amounts of fresh air and light. They grow quickly from seed and propagate readily, but are subject to damping off and if the right balance of light, temperature, and watering is not achieved, they can be easily lost. When grown to perfection they make a stunning show.

Ophrys is a genus of orchids known as bee orchids that are found widely distributed throughout Europe. They can grow in a variety of soils and are particularly common on chalky downs. They are equally at home in an undisturbed herbaceous border, on a rough piece of ground, or in small pots of well-drained soil in the alpine house.

Dactylorhiza praetermissa is another native European species which will adapt to a wide range of garden soils but, like other orchids, it is best naturalized in rough undisturbed ground as it has a dislike of artificial fertilizers. Over a number of years, colonies of these plants will produce seed and increase in size.

Cypripedium calceolus, like its tropical cousins, is scarce in cultivation as it is extremely slow to propagate or raise from seed. Once these slipper orchids have been established they will grow into large clumps, producing beautiful flowers. They are among the hardiest of orchids, being found way up in the Arctic Circle, in northern Canada. Other related species are found in northern Russia. They will do equally well in large flower pots or herbaceous borders.

Above:
Disa uniflora.

Further

Information

Index

ORCHIDS – A CARE MANUAL

Acknowledgments

Front Cover: **Photos Horticultural**
Back Cover: **Octopus Publishing Group Ltd.**/Mark Winwood

A–Z Botanical Collection 106 Bottom Left, /Julia Hancock 26, /M.P. Land 103 Bottom Center Left, /Jiri Loun 91 Bottom, /Dan Sams 106 Bottom Right, /Martin Stankewitz 99, /Malkolm Warrington 103 Bottom Left
Adrian Bloom Horticultural Library/Javier Delgado 56–57, 59 Left, 61
Eric Crichton 69 Top, 86 Top Right, 90 Bottom Right, 102, 103 Top Left
DAC Photographics 8, 24 Right, 52 Right, 60 Top, 62 Top Left, 65 Top, 65 Bottom, 66–67, 74 Top, 75 Top Left, 82, 86 Top Left, 88, 94 Top Left, 94 Top Right, 95 Bottom, 96 Top, 96 Bottom, 97 Bottom, 100 Top, 101 Top Left, 103 Top Center Left, 105 Left, 105 Right, 106 Top Left, 122-123.
Garden Picture Library/Lamontagne 69 Bottom
Garden & Wildlife Matters 96 Center, /Sam North 62 Bottom Right
Octopus Publishing Group Ltd./John Sims 59 Right, /Mark Winwood Endpapers, 1, 2–3, 4–5, 6–7, 9, 10–11, 12, 13, 14, 15 Top Right, 15 Bottom Left, 15 Bottom Right, 16, 17, 18–19, 20 Left, 20 Top Right, 20 Center Right, 20 Bottom Right, 21 Left, 21 Right, 23, 24 Left, 25 Top Right, 25 Center Right, 25 Bottom, 27 Top, 27 Bottom Right, 29, 30–31, 32, 33 Top, 33 Bottom, 34 Top, 34 Bottom, 35, 36, 37 Top Left, 37 Top Right, 37 Bottom Left, 37 Bottom Right, 38, 39 Top Left, 39 Top Center, 39 Top Right, 39 Center Left, 39 Center, 39 Center Right, 39 Bottom Left, 39 Bottom Center, 39 Bottom Right, 41 Top Left, 41 Top Center, 41 Top Right, 41 Center Left, 41 Center, 41 Center Right, 41 Bottom Left, 41 Bottom Center, 41 Bottom Right, 42–43, 44 Top Right, 44 Bottom Left, 45, 47, 48, 49, 50, 51 Right, 51 Top Left, 51 Center Left, 51 Bottom Left, 52 Left, 53, 54 Left, 54 Right, 70 Top Left, 70 Bottom Left, 70 Bottom Right, 71, 75 Top Right, 75 Bottom Left, 75 Bottom Right, 77 Top, 77 Bottom, 78, 79 Top, 79 Bottom Left, 79 Bottom Right, 81, 83 Top, 83 Bottom, 85, 86 Bottom, 87 Top, 87 Bottom, 89, 91 Top, 93, 94 Bottom Left, 95 Top, 97 Top, 100 Bottom, 101 Top Right, 101 Bottom, 109, 111, 112, 113 Left, 113 Right, 118 Top
Harpur Garden Library/Jerry Harpur 27 Bottom Left, 107
E.A.S. la Croix 55, /Dr L Vogelpoel 121
N.H.P.A./Stephen Dalton 63, /E. A. Janes 58
Oxford Scientific Films/Marshall Black 90 Top Left, /Deni Bown 118 Bottom, /Alan & Sandy Carey 40, /Michael Fogden 117,
Kew Orchid Fund/Dr H Pfennig 103 Right
Science Photo Library/Dr Jeremy Burgess 60 Bottom

Photographs

Front cover: *Laeliocattleya* Ocarina
Back cover: *Cymbidium* Sarah Jean
Page 1: *Cattleya trianae*
Pages 2–3: *Coelogyne cristata*
Pages 4–5: *Cymbidium* Sarah Jean
Pages 6–7: *Dendrobium* Stardust
Pages 10–1: A greenhouse full of pale blue *Vanda coerulea* at the start of the 20th century
Pages 18–9: *Phalaenopsis* plant
Pages 30–1: Pseudobulbs
Pages 42–3: *Dendrobium aureum*
Pages 56–7: Cymbidium care
Pages 66–7: *Miltoniopsis*
Pages 122–3: *Cymbidium* Ming Pagoda